D1190403

Beyond Abortion

The Theory and Practice of the Secular State

BEYOND ABORTION

The Theory and Practice of the Secular State

by
CHARLES
E.
RICE

The controversy surrounding the abortion situation in our country is intensifying daily. The Supreme Court and the Catholic Church have been thrust into the spotlight by pro-abortion advocates, confusion reigns. Many of those opposed to abortion treat it as primarily a legal problem, as though it could be solved by merely tinkering with the constitution. They blame the present day abortion laws in effect solely on the U.S. Supreme Court. In fact, the Supreme Court abortion rulings were the inevitable result of the growth and dominance of positivism and secular humanism in American law and the prevalence of the contraceptive ethic in American society.

Pro-life activists will find this work invaluable in showing *why* the abortion battle began and the direction it is heading in. The author sets out to put abortion in its proper context by tracing its development, its future direction, and what can be done to restore the right to live in our law and institutions. Legis-

(continued on page 60)

Beyond Abortion

The Theory and Practice of the Secular State

by

Charles E. Rice

FRANCISCAN HERALD PRESS

1434 WEST 51st STREET • CHICAGO, 60609

Library of Congress Cataloging in Publication Data

Rice, Charles E
  Beyond abortion.

  1. Abortion—United States. 2. Abortion—Law
and legislation—United States. 3. Secularism—
United States. 4. Church and state—United States.
I. Title.
HQ767.5.U5R5   301   78-16248
ISBN 0-8199-0696-4

*REF
HQ
767.5
.U5
R5*

NIHIL OBSTAT:
    Edward A. Malloy, C.S.C.
    Censor Librorum

IMPRIMATUR:
    ✠ William E. McManus
        Most Rev. Ordinary Diocese of Fort Wayne-South Bend

    February 20, 1978   *REF*

    875 43980

MADE IN THE UNITED STATES OF AMERICA

*To my wife, Mary, and our children,
John Laurence, Mary Frances, Anne
Patricia, Joseph Patrick, Charles
Peter, Jeanne Elizabeth, Theresa Helen,
Kathleen Bernadette, Ellen Mary and
Patricia Mary*

Contents

1

The Golden Age Center

Picture this scene, a few years hence:

The vote of the Review Committee was 3 to 0. The Doctor, who was secretary of the meeting, marked the patient's card "MR" and added his initials and the date. This "Merciful Release" had been provided by the Congress almost two years ago in the Geriatric Welfare Act of 1996, which was part of an overall revision of the bankrupt Social Security system.

Under the law, Social Security retirement benefits were reduced by the full amount of any outside income received from whatever source. The only persons, therefore, who actually received Social Security benefits were those whose outside earnings, gifts from relatives, and other income totaled less than the ordinary Social Security benefits. As a result, only the poor received Social Security retirement checks. But still there were too many of them. The Geriatric Welfare Act of 1996 provided that each recipient of Social Security retirement benefits over the age of 65 who was "confined to any hospital or infirmary" for more than three consecutive days "shall be entitled to a Merciful Re-

1

lease on his or her own request or on a decision by the
Review Committee that prolongation of life is a meaningless burden."

The patient was a 71-year-old retired carpenter. His arth-
ritis, thought the Doctor, was what did him in. He had been
assigned to the infirmary in the Golden Age Center for
"observation" when he became unable to work effectively
at his trade. The Geriatric Welfare Act provided that recipients of retirement benefits "are encouraged to be use-
fully engaged at a task of social significance" for at least
the equivalent of three full days a week.

The patient's wife was in good health for her age. Her
four-hour a day job in a public school cafeteria was socially
significant. She was therefore not a total burden on society.
The couple had two grown sons. Both were married with
children of their own and had declined to contribute to
their parents' support. "We love them," said the elder son,
"but we have to look out for our own. Let nature take
its course."

The Doctor returned to the examining room, where the
patient sat in his infirmary gown. He ushered the patient
into an adjoining treatment room "for further tests." There,
another Doctor on duty would administer the Merciful
Release by injection. Because the patient was not in severe
pain and had expressed no wish to die, his widow would
be informed that he had "passed away unexpectedly in his
sleep." In a few days, she would be asked to report to the
Golden Age Center for "consultation." They would explain
to her that she had the option to choose a Merciful Release
for herself. They would explain its advantages for a lonely
widow. A surprising number of spouses chose that course.

The Doctor sometimes wondered whether all this was
wrong. But it was, after all, the law. And its beneficiaries
would be better off with a Merciful Release than they would
be struggling on the borderline of poverty. There were too
many old, poor people. Social Security could not support
them because there were too few young wage earners. Since
1973, more than a million future wage earners had been

eliminated each year from the labor force by abortion. The birth rate was too low to make up the shortage. By 1976, the United States had achieved what the experts called "the perfect contraceptive society." In the latter seventies, sterilization became the most popular form of contraception. In one marriage in three, at least one partner had been sterilized. With sterilization, there is no tomorrow for child-bearing. The popularity of sterilization guaranteed that there would be no sharp increase in the birth rate.

In 1977, five states relaxed their euthanasia laws to provide for voluntary "death with dignity." It was all in the name of individual rights and all for the benefit of the patient. Predictably, however, the shift came from the voluntary withdrawal of life support from the terminally ill to the presumption that the senile and other incompetents would want such release were it available to them. Then the involuntary killings began. The change was hardly noticed. In part this was because Americans had become, in Archbishop Fulton J. Sheen's words, "a violent people." They had "lost a sense of the sacredness of life. There is a love of death, injury and hurting."[1] A psychiatrist described the violence by fans at athletic contests as used "not as a means to an end, but for recreational purposes, for pleasure. It's an end in itself."[2]

When permissive abortion was first advanced in 1967, its proponents masked their campaign under the pretense that the unborn child was something other than a human being. As if the living offspring of human parents could be anything but human. The American people were confused. The Supreme Court kept up this pretense in *Roe v. Wade,* its 1973 abortion ruling, when it said that the unborn child, even in the third trimester of gestation, was at most only "potential life." As the journal of the California Medical Association had accurately observed in 1970, a new ethic of killing was taking over:

> Since the old ethic has not yet been fully displaced it has been necessary to separate the idea of abortion from the

idea of killing, which continues to be socially abhorrent. The result has been a curious avoidance of the scientific fact, which everyone really knows, that human life begins at conception and is continuous whether intra- or extra-uterine until death. The very considerable semantic gymnastics which are required to rationalize abortion as anything but taking a human life would be ludicrous if they were not often put forth under socially impeccable auspices. It is suggested that this schizophrenic sort of subterfuge is necessary because while a new ethic is being accepted the old one has not yet been rejected.[3]

By the mid-seventies, the proponents of abortion had stopped pretending that the child in the womb was something less than human. The idea took hold that the law should not protect every life, that some lives are not worth living. As Supreme Court Justice Thurgood Marshall wrote in 1977:

The enactments challenged here (cutting off Medicaid payments for abortions) brutally coerce poor women to bear children whom society will scorn for every day of their lives. Many thousands of unwanted minority and mixed race children now spend blighted lives in foster homes, orphanages and "reform" schools. . . . Many children of the poor will sadly attend second-rate segregated schools. . . . And opposition remains strong against increasing AFDC benefits for impoverished mothers and children, so that there is little chance for the children to grow up in a decent environment. . . . I am appalled at the ethical bankruptcy of those who preach a "right to life" that means, under present social policies, a bare existence in utter misery for so many poor and their children.[4]

A British physician, Dr. John Goundry, urged in 1977 that doctors be allowed to give a "demise pill" to elderly patients. The "demise pill," he predicted, "will be obligatory within 50 years. People are horrified by my statements. Today's emotions cannot be equated with how people will think in 2025."[5] The doctor was sharply criticized for his views, but he knew better than his critics. "The economics" of elderly care, he wrote, "are devastating and the standard of care is rapidly falling." But Dr. Goundry's timetable was off. The span from *Roe* v. *Wade,* the abortion decision of 1973, to the Merciful Release was half that time.[6]

Largely, it was a matter of economics, not only in the United States but in other countries as well. As *California Medicine* predicted, "the new demographic, ecological and social realities" were so powerful that they displaced the old ethic with the new. There were too many old folks, too few young workers to support them, and the young were not willing to sacrifice their lifestyle for their elders.

Less visible than money and numbers, however, was a dry rot of the spirit. For two centuries, western philosophers had denied the capacity of the mind to know the truth with certainty. There followed the denial of the capacity to know God. Absolute moral principles were out, relative values were in. When the contraceptive pill appeared in 1957, it was seen as a liberation rather than a curse. The efforts to stem the tide by piecemeal attacks on abortion and euthanasia were fruitless. For these evils are merely symptoms of a deeper disorder. This disorder includes the denial of the intellect through positivism, the denial of God through secularism, and the denial of the goodness of life through the contraceptive mentality.

These errors are leading us to the age of the Merciful Release. They are the subject of this book.

2

Positivism

Suppose you are a member of the House of Representatives in 1996. The Geriatric Welfare Act is on the floor for debate. It would subject to death all aged recipients of Social Security whose lives are officially found to be "meaningless." How would you argue against it? The first thing you might say is that it is unconstitutional, a violation of the Fifth Amendment's guarantee that no person shall be deprived of life without "due process of law." But the act provides that the subject who refuses to request his own Merciful Release shall be presumed incompetent. So if the Review Committee decides to grant him a "merciful" death, it is really carrying out what he would desire if he were competent to choose. A similar presumption of incompetency had been developed by the Supreme Court in a 1987 case upholding the Merciful Release of handicapped patients in public hospitals. For more than fifty years the Constitution had been "the judicial version of it,"[1] or whatever the judges said it was. As a safeguard for the helpless it was a shambles. Clearly, the Geriatric Welfare Act would be upheld by the Supreme Court if it were enacted by Congress. So you could not argue the Constitution, because the Constitution is not there anymore. Or you could argue that to kill the aged is unwise and inexpedient. But that argument, too, is a loser. The bottom line is a money line. In that light, most of them *should* be killed. They are useless eaters, and those who are not could be spared by the Review Committee for a time. And if you argue that we ought to beware that the same fate might befall us in our old age, you would be told that we are secure as long as we are useful. And who in his right mind would want to linger on into an old age of humiliating dependency?

Then, if finally you argue that it is simply wrong to kill the innocent, they would laugh at you. You have no right to impose your morality on others. Morality is personal and each individual must decide for himself. Who are you to say what is right or wrong for others?

If they are right, if morality is wholly personal, then the majority may do as they will with the aged and anyone else. If Congress will not admit that some things are always wrong, that there is a law higher than the state, you might as well save your breath.

An act of Congress, a court decision, and even the Constitution itself are forms of man-made law. Are they subject to a higher law, so that they are void if they violate it?

There are two basic approaches to this question. One is positivism, the theory which affirms the validity of human law provided only that it be duly enacted. The other is a natural-law approach that affirms "there is in fact an *objective moral order* within the range of human intelligence, to which human societies are bound in conscience to conform, and upon which the peace and happiness of personal, national and international life depend."[2]

The crucial question is one of epistemology—the theory of knowledge. If man cannot know the essences of things, then there is no objective rightness or wrongness which he can know. If man cannot really know what is just in a given situation, he cannot criticize any particular course of

action as unjust. Questions of right and wrong will therefore have to be resolved by the political process. If that
process produces a Buchenwald or a *Roe v. Wade,* it cannot
be said to be unjust. Describing Nazi Germany, Gustav
Radbruch said that positivism "disarmed the German jurists
against law of an arbitrary and criminal content."[3]

If one believes that he cannot know reality and that he
therefore cannot know what is right or wrong in a given
situation, he has to be a positivist. This is seen in the
writings of Hans Kelsen (1881–1973), who has been well
described as "the jurist of our century."[4] The author of the
Austrian Constitution of 1920, Kelsen was very influential
in Germany between the two World Wars. Kelsen denied
the possibility of natural law. He rejected what he called
"philosophical absolutism," the "metaphysical view that
there is an absolute reality, i.e., a reality that exists in-
dependently of human knowledge."[5] He felt that the claim
that one can actually know reality, and what is right and
wrong, leads to tyranny through the efforts of the rulers
to impose on the people what they, the rulers, "know" to
be for the people's good.

Instead, he adopted what he called "philosophical relativism," the "empirical doctrine that reality exists only within
human knowledge, and that, as the object of knowledge,
reality is relative to the knowing subject. The absolute, the
thing in itself, is beyond human experience; it is inaccessible
to human knowledge and therefore unknowable." This
"philosophical relativism," in Kelsen's view, leads to democracy and the tolerance of divergent views, because "what
is right today may be wrong tomorrow," and the minority
"must have full opportunity of becoming the majority. Only
if it is not possible to decide in an absolute way what is
right and what is wrong is it advisable to discuss the issue
and, after discussion, to submit to a compromise."[6]

The problem with this, of course, is that when the majority or those who are in control of the political process
decide to oppress a minority, there is neither moral nor
legal recourse. When the positivist is confronted by Ausch-

witz, his only objections are those of utility or esthetics. It is not *useful* to kill millions of Jews, and the tables might be turned on us some day. Or the slaughter is offensive to his sensibilities. He cannot say it is *wrong* because he does not believe he can know what is right or wrong.

Law, according to Kelsen, is a system of coercive rules called "legal norms." These rules are prescribed by the legislator in accord with the "basic norm" or constitution of the community. That basic norm may or may not be in a written constitution. Moreover, it is entirely up to the legislator to decide what the basic norm is and whether any particular enactment is in accord with it. Nor is there any restriction on the content of legal rules. "Any content whatsoever can be legal; there is no human behavior which could not function as the content of a legal norm." The only requirement for a law to be valid and binding is that "it has been constituted in a particular fashion, born of a definite procedure and a definite rule."[7]

The legislator decides what law will be useful and in accord with the basic norm as determined by himself. Once a law is enacted, it is obligatory. There is no higher law of nature or of God, and the ultimate criterion is force. The positive law can do anything. It cannot be criticized as unjust. For justice, according to Kelsen, "is not ascertainable by rational knowledge at all. Rather, from the standpoint of rational knowledge there are only interests and conflicts of interests. . . . Justice is an irrational ideal."[8]

It is worthwhile to examine Kelsen, because his "pure theory of law" is the most clear-cut form of positivism. All positivist systems, however, are characterized, in greater or lesser degree, by the denial of the capacity of human reason to know objective truth and to know what is right and wrong. They are concerned only with what the law is, not with what it ought to be.

The fruits of legal positivism can be seen in the experience of Nazi Germany. Even prior to World War I, positivism was dominant in Germany. "According to this new positivistic jurisprudence, the legislator, and he alone, *creates* the law. Everything prior to legislative enactment is at best 'custom,' but never true law. Thus, law and right became wholly identified, and bare 'legality' takes the place of substantive justice as an ideal."[9] The Weimar Constitution, under which Germany was governed from 1918 to 1933, did not recognize any law higher than itself. Certain principles of the natural law, it is true, were embodied in Weimar constitutional guarantees, but the constitution could be readily changed and it was often disregarded through the enactment of unconstitutional laws. Moreover, the constitution empowered the president to abrogate basic rights in some situations.

"But the greatest obstacle to the recognition of natural law was the doctrine of positivism which equated right and might to begin with and, hence, assigned to the legislator full discretion as to the detailed content or provisions of the law, to the point of injustice, indeed to the point of complete, highhanded arbitrariness. A decision of the Supreme Court of the Reich of November 4, 1927, makes this fully clear: 'The legislator is absolutely autocratic, and bound by no limits save those he has set for himself either in the constitution or in some other laws.'"[10]

Of course, positivism was totally dominant during the Hitler years, from 1933 to 1945. A 1936 decree of the Reich Commissar of Justice epitomized this condition: "A decision of the Fuhrer in the express form of a law or decree may not be scrutinized by a judge. In addition, the judge is bound by any other decisions of the Fuhrer, provided that they are clearly intended to declare law."[11]

The most striking example of Nazi positivism was the extermination program. At first directed against the non-rehabilitatable sick and then extended to Jews, Gypsies, and other political undesirables, it began with an order in a Hitler letter of September 1, 1939, to the doctor and administrator he placed in charge of the program. No law or formal order was issued to authorize it. Yet the German doctors, and especially the psychiatrists, complied with enthusiasm because they had long since accepted the notion that the only life worth living is one that is useful.[12] Nor were they, at least overtly, conscious of doing wrong.

For example, Dr. August Hirt became alarmed at the thought that the Jewish race was about to become extinct and that very few authentic Jewish skeletons and skulls were available for study. He decided that science needed a collection of 150 body casts and skeletons of Jews; so the desired specimens were assembled from concentration camps, specially killed, and preserved for science. This collection and the correspondence pertaining to it were captured by the United States Army at the end of the war. Dr. Hirt, a professor of anatomy at the University of Strassburg, was surprised that his project was regarded as different from the collection of fossils for the Museum of Natural History in New York. Since the state had declared Jews to be non-persons, that apparently settled the matter for him. Similarly, when Dr. Waldemar Hoven was on trial in a Nazi court on charges of having murdered some SS men by poison, the judge proved Dr. Hoven's guilt by feeding the same poison to Russian prisoners of war. When they died with the same symptoms as the SS men, Dr. Hoven's guilt was proved. It apparently never occurred to the judge that he was committing murder to prove murder. The judge, acting for the Nazi state, was the law and murder was whatever the state said it was.

After the Second World War, Gustav Radbruch, who had been Minister of Justice in the Weimar Republic and who had advocated positivism, renounced his former view. "Law," he said in 1945, "is the quest for justice." If enactments or decrees deny people their rights, "they are null and void; the people are not to obey them, and jurists must find the courage to brand them unlawful."[13] The German courts, after World War II, freely applied natural-law principles in holding the legislature subject to a higher law.

In the closing months of the war, for instance, a young German soldier was absent without leave. For this offense, an officer shot him without any form of trial and secretly buried the corpse. After the war, the victim's mother sought to recover damages from the officer for the death of her son. The officer pleaded that he was justified by the so-called *Katastrophen* order of Adolf Hitler, authorizing any member of the armed forces to kill instantly any coward, traitor, or deserter. As it turned out, the *Katastrophen* order had not been properly promulgated and therefore did not apply; but the court held that the order could not be a defense even if it had been validly promulgated. The "positive legislative act," said the court, "loses all obligatory power if it violates the generally recognized principles of international law or the natural law."[14]

Any legal system that rests on a denial of the capacity of the mind to know objective truth must be described as positivistic. It will ultimately entrust the liberties of people to a political process that is unencumbered by higher moral restraints.

An example is the utilitarianism of Jeremy Bentham (1748-1832), who said the purpose of the law is to achieve the greatest good of the greatest number. The "good" is defined in terms of pleasure. Man's "only object," wrote Bentham, "is to seek pleasure and to shun pain. . . . Evil is pain, or the cause of pain. Good is pleasure, or the cause of pleasure."[15] Of course, the majority determines what ought to be done to achieve the greatest good for the greatest number. And there is no ground on which one can criticize a law as unjust, for Bentham did not believe that man could know objective right or wrong. "I employ the words just, unjust, moral, immoral, good, bad, simply as collective terms including the ideas of certain pains or pleasures." In his view, "moral good is good only by its tendency to produce physical good. Moral evil is evil only by its tendency to produce physical evil; but when I say physical, I mean the pains and pleasures of the soul as well as the pains and pleasures of the senses."[16]

For the positivist, the principle of utility is the sole rationale for legislation. Man has no intrinsic worth. His only end is the attainment of pleasure and the avoidance of pain. But if his existence inflicts pain on the community—that is, if he is a nuisance—there is no reason why he must be endured. Ultimately, his value is not in what he is but in what he does. "Producers" are tolerated; "useless eaters" are given a merciful release. The Supreme Court abortion rulings are in this respect no different from Auschwitz and Buchenwald. Those rulings, furthermore, are not a sudden aberration in American law. As we shall see in chapter 6, positivism has long been the dominant legal philosophy in the United States.

A positivist will generally be one of two types.[17] One type begins by denying his capacity to know anything beyond an empirical knowledge of individual things. This arid skepticism restricts the mind to the collection and empirical verification of data without coming to any knowledge of the nature of things. The skeptic says, "Nothing is certain." But this is absurd, because he claims to know at least one thing for certain: that nothing is certain. "I tell you truly that we cannot know what is true." Or the empiricist will say that, apart from mathematics and formal logic, a statement of fact is meaningful only if it can be empirically verified by observation.[18] But this statement of "fact" is not empirically verifiable. The skeptic or empiricist is an agnostic, claiming that God, too, is unknowable. He will be a secularist in his view of society and the state. He will tend to be a materialist and will be receptive to the evolution of man. And he will be a positivist because of his claimed inability to know objective truth.

The second type of positivist begins with materialism. Nothing exists but matter. There is no personal, spiritual Creator; no free will, no free spiritual intellect. "Soul" is a mere label we use for the material activities of the brain. History is the story of the development of matter, explained by one theory or another.

For the materialist, there are no absolute truths. There is no right or wrong, and the idea of justice has no meaning. The state is a wholly natural product of the evolution of social forces or other material elements. The positive law is fixed by the state without reference to any higher standard. Law is whatever the state decrees, and the essence of law is force. He is therefore a positivist.

A skeptic or empiricist may or may not deny the existence of God and the spiritual soul. He is agnostic and therefore a positivist. But the materialist, who begins by denying the spirit and God, is not an agnostic. He claims to *know* there is no God and no spirit. He is a positivist because the world is an animal kingdom and might makes right.

In both cases, the skeptic and the materialist will attempt the impossible task of constructing a world without God.

3

Secularism

"We feel like a champagne dinner in honor of the United States Supreme Court for its January [1973] decision on abortion," wrote Paul Blanshard and Edd Doerr in *Humanist* magazine.[1] They correctly described the legalization of abortion as a victory for secular humanism, a faith which "sees man as a product of this world—of evolution and human history—and acknowledges no supernatural purposes."[2]

The secularist *has* to favor permissive abortion, for he is a materialist. There is no God. The world of the spirit does not exist. Man is merely an animal, with no more essential worth than a chimpanzee. There are, therefore, no intrinsic limits to what can be done to man by the state or by other men. The secularist may balk, on esthetic or practical grounds, at the killing of unborn children or others. But he will have no enduring objection to it and will ultimately approve it, at least to some extent.

Today, there are two basic forms of secularism. They are Marxism and secular humanism. The former is the creed of the Communist world. The latter is the official religion of the United States, as we shall see in chapter 7.

18

BEYOND ABORTION

Of the two, Marxism is more fully developed. It is worth sketching its basic concepts, the more easily to see that, in truth, it is a religion.

The Marxist views history as moving according to the immutable laws of dialectical materialism. History is the movement of matter and the dominant matter, as far as society is concerned, is the process of economic production. According to the Marxist laws of history, the existence of private property gives rise to classes. The existence of classes gives rise to the state. At any stage of history, the state is an instrument for the enforcement of the will of the dominant class against the subordinate classes. If there were no classes there would be no state. The character of each age is determined by the dominant mode of economic production and the class which controls that mode will be the dominant class at that time. History develops by a dialectical process, wherein a thesis is contradicted by an antithesis, and the result is a synthesis, or combination of the two theses, on a higher level. This synthesis in turn becomes a new thesis, to be challenged by a new antithesis. This dialectic, with its rejection of immutable truth, is an explanation of all nature as well as history. "Truth" evolves according to fixed material laws.

The Marxist says there are five phases of human history. The first is primitive society, where there was no private property and therefore no class conflict and therefore no state. Soon, however, private property arose, and one of the first forms of private property to become dominant was property in other people.

The second stage, the slave society, in which slaveholding was the dominant form of production, was characterized by class division and the emergence of the state. The slaveholding class, a thesis, was challenged by the landed interests, an antithesis.

The resulting synthesis was the third stage, feudal society, in which the ownership and control of land was the dominant form of production but in which influences of the slave society remained—for example, in the status of the

serfs who were bound to the land. The landed interests
in feudal society were in turn challenged by the mercantile
interests.

The resulting synthesis was the fourth stage of human
history, capitalist or bourgeois society. Here the capitalistic
mode of production was dominant but the ruling capitalist
class was challenged by the proletariat, or factory workers.
As a result of the class struggle between the capitalists
and the proletariat, a new intermediate period was ushered
in. This period is the "dictatorship of the proletariat" or
socialist society. During this time, the proletariat will rule
under the absolute dictation of the Communist Party, which
is the vanguard of the proletariat. The rule of distribution
of goods during this period will be "from each according
to his ability, to each according to his work." By a process
of economic organization, education, and repression, the
dictatorship of the proletariat will mold the new Communist
man. Crucial to this development is the abolition of private
property. Since private property is the cause of division into
classes and since classes lead to class conflict and class
conflict leads to the state, the elimination of property will
eliminate classes and the state itself.

The fifth and final stage of history, therefore—to be brought
about by the dictatorship of the proletariat—will be the
Communist society, in which the state will have withered
away because there is no property and, therefore, there
are no classes to cause class conflict. The only purpose of
the state at any stage is to enforce the will of the dominant
class. In the future Communist society, however, there will
be no state and the rule of distribution will be "from each
according to his ability, to each according to his need."
There is no Communist society today. The Soviet Union
is said to be in the socialist stage, while the United States
is in the capitalist-bourgeois stage.

These theories are an amalgam of Karl Marx (1818–1883),
Friedrich Engels (1820–1895), and Vladimir Ilyich Lenin
(1870–1924). Since Marx's predictions about the failure of
capitalism proved grossly inaccurate, Lenin modified the

theory by substituting the imperialist countries for the capitalistic factory owners and the underdeveloped nations for the proletariat.

Many aspects are omitted from this bare sketch, but two points should be noted. One is that the denial of God is central to the Marxist theory. "The Communists have self-assurance and confidence because of their belief that they can know and eventually control everything because there is no God and no Creation."[3] Or as former Communist Whitaker Chambers said, "The crux of this matter is the question whether God exists. If God exists, a man cannot be a Communist, which begins with the rejection of God. But if God does not exist, it follows that Communism, or some suitable variant of it, is right."[4]

The second point about Marxism is the relativity of truth. However, the Marxist is not a total relativist. He claims to know some truth; but nothing is absolute except the dialectical process. The only truth is that which serves the revolution. "We say," wrote Lenin, "that our morality is entirely subordinated to the interests of the class struggle of the proletariat."[5]

In George Orwell's *1984*, O'Brien, the interrogator, tells Winston:

> You believe that reality is something objective, external, existing in its own right. You also believe that the nature of reality is self-evident. When you delude yourself into thinking that you see something, you assume that everyone else sees the same thing as you. But I tell you, Winston, that reality is not external. Reality exists in the human mind and nowhere else. Not in the individual mind, which can make mistakes, and in any case soon perishes; only in the mind of the Party which is collective and immortal. Whatever the Party holds to be truth *is* truth. It is impossible to see reality except by looking through the eyes of the Party.[6]

O'Brien holds up four fingers and continues, "How many fingers am I holding up, Winston?" "Four." "And if

the Party says that it is not four but five—then how many?"
When Winston says "Four," he is jolted with an electric
shock.

Secular humanism is the other materialist religion. It lacks
the finely wrought orthodoxy of Marxism, but its roots are
similar. The Humanist Manifesto, proclaimed in 1933 by
humanist leaders (including John Dewey), declared, among
other things, that "religious humanists" believe the universe
is "self-existing and not created," that "man is a part of
nature and that he has emerged as the result of a continuous process," and that "the traditional dualism of mind
and body must be rejected." In 1973, a group of philosophers, scientists, and other intellectuals issued an updated
Humanist Manifesto II which reaffirms these ideas and
states that "moral values derive their source from human
experience." The manifesto also supports the "right" to
birth control, abortion, divorce, unrestricted sexual behavior
between consenting adults, "an individual's right to die with
dignity, euthanasia and the right to suicide."[7] Among the
signers were Dr. Alan F. Guttmacher, president of the
Planned Parenthood Federation of America, and B. F.
Skinner, the psychologist who wrote *Beyond Freedom and
Dignity,* a basic manual of behavior modification.

"In the evolutionary pattern of thought," wrote Sir Julian
Huxley, "there is no longer either need or room for the
supernatural. The earth was not created; it evolved."[8] For
the secular humanist, not only is man a product of evolution, so also is truth. Huxley rejected "all belief in Ab-
solutes, whether the absolute validity of moral commandments, of authority of revelation, of inner certitude, or of
divine inspiration."[9] "We ask," said humanist Barbara
Wootton, "no longer what is pleasing to God but what is
good for men."[10]

Since everyone needs God, the secular humanist will substitute another "certainty" for the rejected God. This may
be democracy, utility, the class struggle—whatever. But because he cannot know the essence of anything, he sees no
essential meaning in any reality, including his substitute

gods. Since they are meaningless, they are bound to fail him, and he will be driven to become his own god. As an atheistic existentialist, he will see no purpose or meaning even in himself. He knows that he exists, but *what* he is he cannot say. His only concern will be his own existence—his feelings and his will. This attitude is fairly common among American youth.

As his own god, a young man will tend to regard anything outside himself, especially another person who makes claims upon him, as a rival god and, therefore, an enemy. The anti-life mentality comes easily to him. "Humanism (existentialist, rationalist, empiricist, etc.) always ends in a nihilistic denial of and hatred for reality. It believes in 'nothing, past, present or future.' It holds that 'Life is an absurd torment' and the 'beginning of wisdom is to believe in no truth or wisdom.'"[11] One's hostility to life ultimately embraces his own life. The logical end, as Albert Camus indicated, is suicide,[12] for man "cannot live without faith, and the collapse of false faiths is productive of strongly suicidal tendencies in modern man."[13]

This nihilistic tendency is not peculiar to secular humanism; it is inherent in all types of secularism, including the Marxist variety. The root fallacy is the denial that man can know reality and God. When the substitute god fails, as it is bound to do, secular man is left with nothing but himself, alone in a meaningless world.

Secularism, like positivism, necessarily leads to the total state. Rene Descartes (1596-1650) concluded that the only thing he could not doubt was his own existence. *"Cogito ergo sum:* I think, therefore I am." Man can know with certainty nothing outside himself. We find this idea that the external world is unknowable in Immanuel Kant (1724-1804), who taught that we cannot know the *noumena,* or things as they really are. All we can know are *phenomena,* the appearance of things. We can only know things as they appear to us subjectively. Jeremy Bentham logically concluded that utility is the purpose of the law because there are no objective and knowable standards which the law must

follow. Yet, as with Descartes, man is not really concerned
with anything outside himself. Pleasure and pain are all that
matter. Hedonism is the rule. However, somebody has to
give the orders or society will fall apart. Thus we reach
Hans Kelsen's "Pure" theory of law, under which the
law is the law. It must be obeyed and it is irrational to
ask whether it is right or wrong.

The legatees of this denial of the intellect and of God
are the totalitarians. The Nazis knew what they were about.
They were dogmatic and they exploited the disorder created
by secularistic positivism. The Marxist-Leninists, too, are
dogmatic. The dictatorship of the proletariat will mold
man so that he will want to live as Communist man, without God and without the state. But the Communist fantasy
of the withering away of the state will never happen. The
reality is the total dictatorship of the proletariat, led by the
Communist Party.

This book is concerned with the anti-life society and the
total state it generates; but it is clear that the only protection for innocent life is society's recognition of God.
Denial that man can know God involves a denial that he
can know spiritual reality, including the abstract essences
of things. If man cannot know spiritual reality, it is because
he has no spiritual soul and no spiritual intellect. He is
merely matter. If he is not spiritual, he cannot know that
anything is inherently right or wrong, and it is all downhill
from there. "Communism," said Alexander Solzhenitsyn,
"has infected the whole world with a belief in the relativity
of good and evil" and has persuaded "all of us that those
concepts are old fashioned and laughable. But if we are to
be deprived of the concepts of good and evil, what will
be left? Nothing but the manipulation of one another. We
will sink to the status of animals."[14] The secular humanists
and positivists can oppose only the excesses of Communists.
They are all philosophical brothers under the skin.

The Communist is a positivist in that whatever the party
dictates is the truth. And he is of course a secularist. The

affinity between the secular humanist and the Marxist arises from the fact that both are materialist. Neither recognizes God and his law. As for man, he is not a person with a spiritual soul and an eternal destiny; he is instead a piece of flotsam or jetsam thrown up for a brief time in the void. Man is to be manipulated for the dominant ends of the secular society. In the United States, those ends are technological and man tends to become a cog in the machine. As John Cardinal Wright put it, a choice between Marxist dialectical materialism and "the mentality of automation and computerized controls" would be no choice but only "secular humanism" with two forms of materialism, "neither entirely distinct from the other." We become dialectical materialists in all but name, he said, if we ignore that "whole universe of values and realities that cannot be reduced to statistics, to handy little formulae, for feeding into computers" and if, "prescinding from divine faith, we accept the lie that nothing is valid or true which does not admit of demonstration from human experience or mechanical analysis."[15]

It is clear that the two contending forces are secularism (of whatever variety) and the religion of Christ. There is no peaceful co-existence between them. Secularism, whatever the variety, is a fighting faith. Because no one can live without a god, secularists are not content to dismiss God and ignore him thereafter. They must displace him with a new god, whether history, the state, or man himself. "One of the main things needed by the world today is a new single religious system," wrote humanist Sir Julian Huxley.[16]

Since the true God is not a quitter, the secularists have a continuing fight on their hands. They *have* to be militant. The conflict is especially acute on the issue of life itself. Marxists support anti-life policies because they undermine the capitalist-imperialist society. Secular humanists support them because man is no more than a barnyard animal to be manipulated. However, the recent victories of secularism "could not have occurred," said humanist Barbara Wootton, "had not dogmatic religious belief been on the wane."[17]

One reason for the decline in religious belief is the triumph in this country of the secularist dogma that religion (except for secularism itself) is a matter of private preference with no relevance to the public life of the nation. Since secularism is the official religion of our country, the public climate is therefore no longer supportive of those who want to practice their belief in God and transmit it to their children. The public climate is hostile to all theistic belief, but especially to the Catholic Church. The Supreme Court's abortion ruling, said Blanshard and Doerr, was "the most direct defeat for the Catholic hierarchy in the history of American law." And so it was. The Catholic hierarchy, whatever its faults, is the custodian of the Truth of Christ. And the Catholic Church is the one which is preeminently capable of resisting the anti-life movement without compromise, not only in its excesses but also on its basic philosophy. Archbishop John Murphy of Wales once predicted that "in some secular humanistic future, when the only sin will be pain, the only evil ill health; when childbearing will be looked upon as a disease, and terminal illnesses will not be tolerated; when it is just possible that the free, human beings will be forbidden to have a child, or a smoke, or a drink, save by prescription of the National Health; in that cold, clinical future, you will search in vain for the rebels save in the ranks of the Catholic Church."[18]

4

St. Thomas Aquinas

Christopher Derrick once said the basic question is whether "pigs is pigs."[1] Are we capable of knowing what makes a pig a pig? Can we know that there is a difference in essence and species between a pig and a horse? Or is the word "pig" merely an arbitrary term we use to describe this particular animal, which, for all we know, may some day evolve into a horse? "Pig" is an abstract idea, expressing the concept which describes all members of that species. "Justice" is also an abstract idea. Can we know what is just and what is unjust? Are some actions always unjust, no matter what the subjective culpability or lack of it of the person who performs them? Is there an objective order, according to which some acts will always be "just," in the same way that some animals will always be members of the species we call "pigs"? Can we really know that objective order? Going one step further, can we really know that there is a God? Can we know his attributes?

Postivism denies the power of the intellect to know truth. Because no one can know what is right or wrong, it leaves the resolution of such questions to the state. Secularism denies God. It sees no life beyond the grave and regards man as a material animal to be manipulated and controlled. As we shall see in chapters 6 and 7, positivism and secularism are dominant in American law. But before we examine what our Constitution was meant to do, and how it has failed, we should look at the realistic philosophy of law advanced by St. Thomas Aquinas (1225–1274).

St. Thomas, according to Pope Paul VI, "holds the principal place" among the doctors of the Church.[2] His teaching meets and defeats positivism and secularism at every point. If this book merely recited what is wrong with the world, it would be negative and hopeless. Instead, we ought to reassure ourselves at this point that there is a philosophy which includes—but goes beyond—a refutation of errors. It offers a common-sense view of reality, human nature, and the law.

The foundation of any realistic philosophy is the capacity of man to know the essences of things. Man understands essences through his senses and his intellect. He perceives individual things through his senses and imagination, and through his intellect he knows the essences of those things:

> Each person has his own intellect which has two functions: it abstracts essences from sense-perceived individuals; this abstracted essence is then intelligible; it is impressed on the passive intellect. On reflection the passive intellect understands that one essence belongs to many individuals, forming a class which can again be further unified by still more abstract ideas into wider classes. Abstraction terminates in the idea of being which includes God, the only self-existent Being. "I am who I am."[3]

Man therefore understands by means of his senses and intellect. There is nothing in the intellect that has not first been in the senses. A thing is not known through the senses alone, but through the intellect with the aid of the senses. The intellect abstracts or takes into itself the thing in its essence, in that which it is. In making a judgment, the intellect performs a spiritual function, asserting that "This is a book" rather. than "This is a baseball." It is a spiritual function because the abstract idea of "bookness" does not exist in itself as a material thing. It is a universal idea—that is, an idea of those characteristics which are the essence of that species we call books. That book exists whether we think about it or not, and it is a book even if we mistakenly call it a baseball or an elephant.

The mind is able "to attain certain and unchangeable truth,"[4] but the "human mind is able to understand only by remaining in contact with reality; by continually adjusting its knowledge to reality."[5] For truth is the conformity of a statement with reality, "the agreement of the assertion expressed in the judgment with the actual reality."[6] If I say that the book is an elephant, my statement is untrue, no matter how sincerely I may believe that is an elephant. Extending this further, if I say that contraception is good, my statement is false, no matter how sincere I am.

Following Aristotle's lead, St. Thomas distinguishes three acts of the intellect.[7] The first is simple apprehension or intellection, expressing itself in one concept or idea, for example, "dog." The second act of the intellect is judgment, "a simple cognitive action in which something is known to be in a certain manner, or not to be so." "Lassie is a dog" is a judgment, but whether it is true or false will depend on whether it conforms to reality. If Lassie is in fact a dog, the statement is true. The third act of the intellect is discursive reasoning or ratiocination. The syllogism would be the typical example: All men are mortal; John is a man; therefore, John is mortal.

The notion of a natural law, knowable to the intellect and higher than the state or the people, is not a Catholic phenomenon. Aristotle wrote of "natural justice."[8] Cicero believed that true "law is the distinction between things just and unjust, made in agreement with that primal and most ancient of all things, Nature."[9] "If the principles of Justice were founded on the decrees of peoples, the edicts of princes, or the decisions of judges, then Justice would

sanction robbery and adultery and forgery of wills, in case
these acts were approved by the votes or decrees of the
populace."[10] On the contrary, however, "those who formu-
late wicked and unjust statutes for nations, thereby breaking
their promises and agreements, put into effect anything
but 'laws.' It may thus be clear that in the very definition
of the term 'law' there inheres the idea and principle of
choosing what is just and true."[11] Cicero, the Roman, has
been described as "the channel through which the theory of
natural law flowed from Greeks to Early Christians, and
then on to great mediaeval Schoolmen."[12]

St. Thomas' most significant philosophical achievement
was "his successful integration of Christian theology and
Greek, or perhaps better, Aristotelian philosophy."[13] In
this he was greatly indebted to St. Augustine (354–430),
who integrated legal philosophy and theology and who
insisted that "theological-Christian considerations not only
permeate the whole of law and legal theory, but in fact
constitute the only sound foundation of true law and true
jurisprudence."[14] St. Thomas, following St. Augustine, understood and affirmed the order in the universe. The world
is not a product of chance. Rather it was created by a
loving God whose existence and attributes we can demon-
strate and who has ordered his creation in accord with his
design. God, the Creator, has a plan for the world. A
"universal rational orderliness" is "characteristic of the
whole universe."[15] The "whole community of the universe
is governed by Divine Reason. Wherefore the very Idea of
the government of things in God the Ruler of the universe,
has then the nature of a law."[16] This law, "the Divine
Reason's conception of things," is called by St. Thomas
the eternal law.

Just as the maker of an automobile has built into it a
certain nature (it drives, it does not fly) and gives directions
for its use so that it will achieve its end, that is, de-
pendable transportation, so God has built a certain nature
into man to follow if he is to achieve his final end, which
is eternal happiness with God in Heaven. These directions

are found in revelation and the natural law. Revelation includes the Old Testament and the New Testament, and St. Thomas calls it the divine law. The divine law is necessary, among other reasons, because "on account of the uncertainty of human judgment, especially on contingent and particular matters, different people form different judgments on human acts; whence also different and contrary laws result. In order, therefore, that man may know without any doubt what he ought to do and what he ought to avoid. it was necessary for man to be directed in his proper acts by a law given by God, for it is certain that such a law cannot err."[17]

In addition to the eternal law and the divine law of revelation, there is a natural law. This exists because man, a rational creature, "has a share of the Eternal Reason, whereby it [the rational creature] has a natural inclination to its proper act and end; and this participation of the eternal law in the rational creature is called the natural law." The "light of natural reason, whereby we discern what is good and what is evil, which is the function of the natural law, is nothing else than an imprint on us of the Divine Light. It is therefore evident that the natural law is nothing else than the rational creature's participation of the Eternal Law."[18] The natural law is therefore a rule of reason, promulgated by God in man's nature, whereby man can discern how he should act.

What are the commands of this natural law and how are they known? Here we should first distinguish the speculative reason from the practical reason. The object of the speculative reason is knowledge, while the object of the practical reason is conduct. The first principle of the speculative reason is the principle of contradiction, that a thing cannot be and not be at the same time under the same aspect. This principle is self-evident and indemonstrable; no rational person can doubt it. The first self-evident principle of the practical reason is that "good is to be done and promoted and evil is to be avoided."[19] The good is that which is in accord with the nature of the thing in question. Thus it is

BEYOND ABORTION

good for man to eat a ham sandwich, and a barbed-wire sandwich is not good for man because the human stomach is not a trash compactor. Similarly, it is good to put gasoline in the tank of an automobile as needed. It is not good to put molasses in the tank, because the nature of an automobile is such that it is not made to run on molasses. In the same way, chastity, according to one's state in life, is good, but adultery is not.

Since the good is to be sought and evil is to be avoided, and since the good is that which is in accord with nature, the next question is: What is the nature of man? The essential nature of man is unalterable, since it is a reflection of the unchanging divine essence.[20] St. Thomas says that "all those things to which man has a natural inclination are naturally apprehended by reason as being good, and consequently as objects of pursuit, and their contraries as evil, and objects of avoidance."[21]

The basic inclinations of man are five:

1. To seek the good, which is ultimately his highest good which is eternal happiness.
2. To preserve himself in existence.
3. To preserve the species, that is, to unite sexually.
4. To live in community with other men.
5. To use his intellect and will, that is, to know the truth and to make his own decisions.[22]

The existence of these inclinations is self-evident. They are put into human nature by God because they help man achieve his final end of eternal happiness. From these inclinations man applies the natural law by deduction. Basically, the syllogism is used: Good should be done; this action is good; this action therefore should be done.[23] However, because of "concupiscence or some other passions . . . evil perversions . . . or . . . vicious customs and corrupt habits," people may come to the wrong conclusions in their understanding or application of the secondary principles of the natural law.[24] For example, among some people, as St. Thomas points out, homosexual activity is not considered sinful although it is specifically stigmatized by St. Thomas as the "unnatural crime."[25]

The fact that people are in error in their perception of the natural law may reduce or eliminate their subjective culpability. But whether or not they are subjectively culpable, such action is always objectively wrong.

There are thus four types of law: eternal law, divine law (revelation), the natural moral law, and, lastly, human law, which is an integral part of God's plan. The human law is designed to promote the common good and help man attain his highest end of happiness with God. The human law is derived from the natural law. It may be derived by conclusion, as the law that one must not kill is a conclusion from the basic "principle that we should do harm to no man";[26] or by determination, for example, "the law of nature has it that the evildoer should be punished," but the human law decrees whether the punishment should be by fine or imprisonment or both.[27]

Human law is framed "for the common good of all the citizens."[28] "The purpose of human law is to lead men to virtue, not suddenly but gradually."[29] But though the law should promote virtue, it should not prescribe every virtue or forbid every vice, lest by its unenforceability the law be drawn into disrepute.

If human laws are just, they bind man in conscience, "from the eternal law whence they are derived, according to Prov. viii 15: By me kings reign, and lawgivers decree just things." But if a human law "deflects from the law of nature," it is unjust and "is no longer law but a perversion of law."[30]

St. Thomas explained that a law may be unjust in two ways:

> *First, by being contrary to human good* . . . either in respect of the *end,* as when an authority imposes on his subjects burdensome laws, conducive, not to the common good, but rather to his own cupidity or vainglory; or in respect of the *author,* as when a man makes a law that goes beyond the power committed to him; or in respect

of the *form,* as when burdens are imposed unequally on the community, although with a view to the common good. The like are acts of violence rather than laws; because as Augustine says (De Lib. Arb. i.5), a law that is not just, seems to be no law at all. Wherefore such laws do not bind in conscience, except perhaps in order to avoid scandal or disturbance, for which cause a man should even yield his right. . . .

Secondly, laws may be unjust through being opposed to the Divine good: such are the laws of tyrants inducing to idolatry, or to anything else contrary to the Divine law; and laws of this kind must nowise be observed, because, as stated in Acts v. 29, we ought to obey God rather than men.[31]

Aquinas is different from the positivists and secularists in two major respects. Most importantly, he places human law in the framework of the overall divine plan. God wants man to achieve eternal happiness by choosing to obey God. The plan of God for man is known through revelation and the natural law. Human law and, therefore, the state exist to promote the common good and thereby to help man achieve his end of eternal happiness with God. The state is not a necessary evil, nor is it a mere contrivance of the majority or some mythical social compact. Rather it is good because it is an integral part of God's plan. But the state is not an end in itself; it is an instrument to help man achieve his end. St. Thomas, of course, had not experienced the modern state, but his discussion of the human law provides the basic principles to govern the state in any age. Aquinas, therefore, directly contradicts the secularist and the positivist by grounding his theory of law on the reality of God. Only in this way can human law be limited. Otherwise, if God is not recognized, the state becomes god.

The second major way that St. Thomas differs from the positivists and secularists is in his view of the nature of law. The positivist and the secularist reduce law to an act of will by the one in control. It is true that there is an element of will in the law (every law is a command), but, as St. Thomas affirms, something more is needed. In order that "what is commanded may have the nature of law, it needs to be in accord with some rule of reason."[32] This requirement proceeds from the fact that "the whole community of the universe is governed by Divine Reason."[33] The divine will cannot act separately from the divine reason because "God cannot be at variance with himself."[34] The essence of law therefore pertains to reason. This is true of the natural law and human law as well as the eternal law and revelation.

It follows from this that there are limits to what the human law can do. If it acts contrary to reason, as found in the eternal law, revelation, and the natural law, that human "law" is simply not a law. It is an act of violence rather than a law.[35] From prudent concern for the common good, we may be morally obliged to obey it to avoid greater evil. But there are situations in which we are not only entitled to disobey a law but bound to do so: "Such are the laws of tyrants inducing to idolatry, or anything else contrary to the Divine law."[36]

Adherence to the teachings of St. Thomas will enable us to ask the right questions. We do not ask whether a human law is for the greatest good of the greatest number. Rather, we ask whether it is in accord with the eternal law, revelation, and the natural law. Through our unaided reason, we would make mistakes and contradict each other in answering that question, but the living God provides the living Church to show us the answers. Through adherence to the magisterium of the Church, that is, the teaching authority of the Pope and the bishops in communion with him, we have the sure guide that unaided reason cannot provide.

According to Aquinas, therefore, there is a real world out there, created by a loving God who wants us to choose to be with him eternally in heaven. We can really know this world and the natures of the things in it, including ourselves. We can really know what is right and what is wrong. If we act according to our nature, especially as assisted by divine revelation through the teaching Church, we shall obtain our final end. Moreover, the human law is part of God's plan. Only through adherence to the natural law and the divine law can a society achieve lasting justice and peace.

5

The Natural Law and the Constitution:
The Original Intent

> We hold these truths to be self-evident, that all men are created equal, that they are endowed by their Creator with certain unalienable Rights, that among these are Life, Liberty and the pursuit of Happiness. That to secure these rights, Governments are instituted among Men, *deriving their just powers from the consent of the governed,* that whenever any Form of Government becomes destructive of these ends, it is the Right of the People to alter or to abolish it, and to institute new Government, laying its foundation on such principles and organizing its powers in such form, as to them shall seem most likely to effect their Safety and Happiness.[1]

If you asked a better-than-average high school student why the United States Constitution is legitimate, he (or she) would probably answer that it was established through the consent of the people. If he were really a good student, he would call to mind the words of the Declaration of Independence about governments' "deriving their just powers from the consent of the governed." Undoubtedly, such consent is one factor in making a government legitimate, but is there something else?

As Edward S. Corwin said, "The attribution of supremacy to the Constitution on the ground solely of its rootage in popular will represents . . . a comparatively late outgrowth of American constitutional theory. Earlier the supremacy accorded to constitutions was ascribed less to their putative source than to their supposed content, to their embodiment of essential and unchanging justice."[2]

If the Constitution owes its legitimacy purely to the consent of the people, that consent must be continually updated because the founding generation had no right to bind future generations without their consent. Government itself will tend to be the arbiter of the terms of that continuing consent. And if consent, rather than content, controls, there can be no inherent limit to the governmental action which can be sanctioned by that consent. The will of the interpreter of the consensus then prevails. The theory that the Constitution is founded solely on the consent of the governed leads necessarily to positivism.

This is no mere academic point. Are there some things that government cannot do, some rights it cannot invade, even if the majority consents?

Despite the popular assumption that consent is the all-sufficient basis for our government, the evidence indicates that there was much more to it. The Ninth Amendment to the Constitution provides that "the enumeration in the Constitution of certain rights shall not be construed to deny or disparage others retained by the people." But, as Corwin observes, these "rights" were drawn from "the principles of transcendental justice." They "owe nothing to their recognition in the Constitution—such recognition was necessary if the Constitution was to be regarded as complete." To appreciate this, we ought to note some historical background.

The notion of a law that is higher than the state and even higher than the people was neither an eighteenth-century nor a Catholic creation. In chapter 4 we saw the development of this idea in Aristotle, Cicero, Augustine, and Aquinas. It later became a feature of the English common law. Sir Edward Coke, in his dictum in Dr.

Bonham's case,[3] concluding that an act of Parliament could not justify the London College of Physicians in punishing Dr. Bonham for practicing medicine in London without a license from the college, said:

> And it appears in our books, that in many cases, the common law will controul Acts of parliament, and sometimes adjudge them to be utterly void: for when an Act of parliament is against common right and reason, or repugnant, or impossible to be performed, the common law will controul it, and adjudge such Act to be void.

That same year, in his report in Calvin's case,[4] Coke described the "law of nature" as "that which God at the time of creation of the nature of man infused into his heart, for his preservation and direction and this is *lex aeterna,* the moral law, called also the law of nature. And by this law, written with the finger of God in the heart of man, were the people of God a long time governed before the law was written by Moses, who was the first reporter or writer of law in the world."

Coke died in 1634. In 1688 the Glorious Revolution deposed James II, established the supremacy of Parliament, and made a profound change in the English law. Coke had interpreted Magna Carta, the agreement of 1215 between King John and the barons, as requiring the invalidation of statutes if they were contrary to "common right and reason." But after 1688 there was no law superior to Parliament.[5] This is seen in William Blackstone's *Commentaries,* first published in 1765, where he generally affirmed the supremacy of the "law of nature," saying that "no human laws are of any validity if contrary to this."[6] But Blackstone was a parliamentary supremacist. Despite his general affirmation of the controlling law of nature, he endorsed the English political reality that nobody had authority to overturn an act of Parliament. He described Parliament as the body "where that absolute despotic power which must in all governments reside somewhere, is entrusted by the constitution of these kingdoms." Parliament, he said, "can

do everything that is not naturally impossible." The "omni-
potence of parliament" is such that "what the parliament
doth, no authority upon earth can undo. . . . So long as
the English constitution lasts, we may venture to affirm,
that the power of parliament is absolute and without
control."[7]

The British government, in the years that led to the
American Revolution, insisted that the law of the land and
the rights of English subjects were whatever Parliament
declared them to be. The Declaration of Independence and
the Revolution itself were a reaction to this parliamentary
positivism. Thus George Mason, in arguing the case of
Robin v. *Hardaway*,[8] cited Coke's statements in Bonham's
case and Calvin's case and declared:

> Now all acts of legislature apparently contrary to natural
> right and justice, are, in our laws, and must be in the na-
> ture of things, considered as void. The laws of nature are
> the laws of God; whose authority can be superseded by
> no power on earth. A legislature must not obstruct our
> obedience to him from those punishments they cannot pro-
> tect us. All human constitutions which contradict his laws,
> we are in conscience bound to disobey. Such have been
> the adjudications of our courts of justice.

The contrast between positivism and the natural-law concept that underlay the Constitution can be seen in James
Otis' pamphlet, *Rights of the British Colonies:*

> To those who lay the foundation of government in force
> and mere brutal power, it is objected, that their system
> destroys all distinction between right and wrong; that it
> overturns all morality . . . leads directly to scepticism and
> ends in atheism. When a man's will and pleasure is his
> only rule and guide what safety can there be either for
> him or against him, but in the point of a sword?
> . . . The common good of the people is the Supreme
> law . . . of nature . . . given to the human race (though
> too many of them are afraid to assert it) by the only

monarch in the Universe Who alone has a clear and indisputable right to absolute power because He is the only one who is omniscient as well as omnipotent.[9]

The evidence is abundant that the American Revolution was directed against parliamentary positivism. Nor was it a question of favoring the executive or judiciary over the legislature. The separation of powers that was built into the Constitution, with its checks and balances among the three branches of government, was designed to ensure that one or two branches of government could not get the upper hand. At the same time, the government of the United States was established with only delegated powers, with the states and the people retaining all the other governmental powers. The Constitution of the United States was the first example in history of a government's creation with only delegated and limited powers. The prior history of liberty had been one of placing curbs on the otherwise unlimited powers of government. And reinforcing the limited delegation in the Constitution was the American concept that government power, as such, is inherently limited by a higher law. The Revolution was not fought for the sake of substituting one unlimited government for another.

Alexander Hamilton, while an undergraduate at King's College (later Columbia University), made this clear when he replied to criticism of the legality of the Continental Congress:

> There are some events in society to which human laws cannot extend, but when applied to them lose their force and efficacy. In short when human laws contradict or discountenance the means which are necessary to preserve the essential rights of any society, they defeat the proper end of all laws and so become null and void. . . . The sacred rights of mankind are not to be rummaged for among old parchments or musty records. They are written as with a sunbeam, in the whole volume of human nature, by the hand of Divinity itself and can never be erased or obscured by mortal power.[10]

Sir Edward Coke's *Institutes,* in which he expounded his concept of a higher law, "were the most authoritative law books available" to eighteenth-century colonial lawyers.[11] But probably no general work had greater influence in popularizing the idea of natural rights in the colonies than John Locke's *Second Treatise of Civil Government.* In this work, published in 1690 to justify the Glorious Revolution of 1688, which deposed King James II, Locke asserted a right of revolution against tyrannical government, whether parliament or king. He said that originally there was a state of nature in which men lived in freedom and peace. But each man was judge in his own case in the absence of a civil authority, and there was no established, known law. To avoid these and other inconveniences, men established government by the "social compact." Civil society is therefore founded on consent. Men establish government "for the mutual preservation of their lives, liberties and estates, which I call by the general name—property. The great and chief end, therefore, of men uniting into commonwealths, and putting themselves under governments, is the preservation of their property; to which, in the state of nature, there are many things wanting."[12]

The legislative power or supreme civil authority, however, is subject to the law of nature and cannot rule by arbitrary decrees, because persons in the state of nature who entered into society had no power to act arbitrarily with respect to themselves or others. They therefore could transfer no such power to the government they created. The rules made by legislators must be "conformable to the law of Nature, i.e., to the will of God, of which that is a declaration."[13] And "the community perpetually retains a supreme power of saving themselves from the attempts and designs of any body, even of their legislators whenever they shall be so foolish or so wicked as to lay and carry on designs against the liberties and properties of the subject."[14] This right of revolution against tyranny is the right of the "community" to regain the powers it delegated to the government and to establish new forms of government. But here we see a weakness of Locke's theory; he is a majoritarian:

> For when any number of men have, by the consent of
> every individual, made a community, they have thereby
> made that community one body, with a power to act as
> one body, which is only by the will and determination of
> the majority . . . and so everyone is bound by that con-
> sent to be concluded by the majority.[15]

The majority could overturn the arbitrary acts of the
government, or the government itself; or the majority could
conclude that the government was not arbitrary. In either
case the will of the majority would control. Locke's supposed higher law of nature provides no real protection and
no ground for attacking as unjust the decisions of the majority. The reason for this failing is that Locke was an
empiricist, who denied that essences, natures, or species
could be known. "Basically a skeptic in metaphysics, Locke
could not attain to certainty in moral philosophy, a prolongation of metaphysics. His moral philosophy, had he
ever worked it out, would have ended in a barren utilitarianism of the Benthamite type."[16]

Despite his emphasis on God and the law of nature,
Locke ends in practically the same position as the analytical
positivist Hans Kelsen. Whatever the majority decrees is
law and binds the minority. No one can say that it is unjust for no one can know what is unjust, where the majority has otherwise ordained. This dominance of the majority is evident in Locke's *Second Treatise of Government*,
which had great influence in the colonies. In this respect,
Locke is inconsistent with the spirit of the American Revolution, which rejected all despotism, whether of parliament,
king, or a majority.

If one follows Locke, one cannot say with certainty what
is right or wrong when the majority says otherwise. The
New England clergy who espoused Lockean ideas said "The
voice of nature is the voice of God"; "Reason and the
voice of God are one"; "Christ confirms the law of nature."

The dictate of reason, as interpreted by the majority, becomes the voice of God. "The point of view," observes Professor Corwin, "is thoroughly deistic; reason has usurped the place of revelation, and without affront to piety."[17] The important point is that the majority determines what is reasonable.

Thomas Hobbes (1588–1679) postulated a state of nature in which men were hostile to one another. By the "social compact," according to Hobbes, man vested the sovereign with virtually unlimited power so as to achieve order. With Locke, the unlimited power "is in the corporate majority, which then determines the form of government."[18]

Thomas Aquinas put human law in the context of a divine order that is knowable to man. Human law must be in conformity with the natural law, which is knowable to reason, with the divine law of revelation providing certitude where reason might fail. Some things are always unjust, no matter what the majority might say. Locke, however, did not see such order in the eternal law, the divine law, the natural law, and the human law. As an empiricist, Locke did not believe he could really know the essence or nature of anything. He denied that one could attain certainty in moral philosophy. So instead of an ordered existence, pursuant to the plan of the divine reason, Locke postulated the fictional situation of isolated individuals milling around in the state of nature. For their convenience— as with Hobbes it was for their safety—they form a society and government. But the only restraint on that government is the consent of the governed, that is, the will of the majority. The state, according to Locke, owes its origin not to the nature of things, according to the divine plan, but to the social contract.[19]

The establishment of the American system on a higher foundation of law is an important practical point. On the one hand, natural-law concepts are applied by the courts, which find them embodied in the Constitution. But it is important to recognize a law which is higher than the Constitution. We need a coherent ground on which to call a law, a court decision, or even the Constitution itself, unjust. The expectation of such criticism on the basis of a higher, enduring standard is itself a brake on despotism. In fact, it is the only brake. Paper guarantees of constitutional rights are not worth the paper they are written on unless there is a conviction among the people that God's law controls and that acts of tyranny are void no matter how carefully they are shrouded in the Constitution. John Locke notwithstanding, this was the evident intent of our Declaration of Independence and our Constitution.

6

The Failure of the Constitution:
Positivism

An insight into the positivist mentality can be gained from the position of Supreme Court Justice William O. Douglas, who concurred in the *Roe* v. *Wade* ruling that an unborn child is a non-person and has no rights. But the year before, he dissented when the Supreme Court ruled that the Sierra Club lacked sufficient interest in the issue to be allowed to sue in federal court to block the Walt Disney Mineral King Park in California.[1] Justice Douglas said that the Sierra Club should be allowed to sue on behalf of "inanimate objects," such as "valleys, alpine meadows, rivers, lakes, estuaries, beaches, ridges, groves of trees, swampland, or even air that feels the destructive pressures of modern technology and modern life." Inanimate objects have rights, according to Justice Douglas: "The voice of the inanimate object, therefore, should not be stilled." Justice Douglas became even more emphatic when discussing the rights of "the pileated woodpecker as well as the coyote and bear, the lemmings as well as the trout in the stream." And he paid special honor to the pupfish, "which are one inch long and are useless to man." (Senator Alan Cranston

[D., Cal.] has introduced a bill to establish a 35,000-acre Pupfish National Monument.) Douglas, who is now retired from the court, quoted the statement of Michael Frome approvingly, that "saving the pupfish would symbolize our appreciation of diversity in God's tired old biosphere, the qualities which hold it together and the interaction of life forms. When fishermen rise up united to save the pupfish they can save the world as well."

The positivist mind in action is wondrous to behold. For Justice Douglas, legalized abortion is "good" because the unborn child has no rights. But trees, trout, and pupfish have rights. So, for whatever reason, killing a pupfish is bad but abortion is good—unless, perhaps, the women were pregnant with a pupfish. But if the pupfish were defective?

The point is not to lampoon Justice Douglas; rather, his opinions in these two cases will help us understand how positivism operates in American law. He is, of course, inconsistent in affirming rights for rocks but not for unborn babies. However, we can say he is inconsistent only if we claim that there is something inherent in an unborn baby that requires that he or she have more rights than a rock or a pupfish. The positivist is unable to make this claim. If one cannot know the essence of a man, one cannot say that his right to live must always be superior to that of a fish.

Positivism is clearly the dominant legal philosophy in the United States. Justice Oliver Wendell Holmes, a leading figure in American jurisprudence, was of the opinion that "truth was the majority vote of the nation that could lick all others."[2] "I wonder," he said, "if cosmically an idea is any more important than the bowels."[3] He defined law as merely "a statement of the circumstances in which the public force will be brought to bear upon men through the courts."[4] Holmes was praised by Justice Benjamin Cardozo as "for all students of the law and for all students of human society the philosopher and seer, the greatest of our age in the domain of jurisprudence and one of the greatest of the ages." Yet Holmes was of the opinion "that the sacredness of human life is a purely municipal ideal of no validity outside the jurisdiction. I believe that force, mitigated so far as may be by good manners, is the *ultima ratio,* and between two groups that want to make inconsistent kinds of world I see no remedy except force."[5]

In *Roe* v. *Wade,* probably the clearest example of triumphant positivism in American law, the Supreme Court said it need not decide whether the unborn child is a human being. Instead, it held that, whether or not he is a human being, he is a non-person and therefore is not entitled to the right to live. The ruling is therefore the same, in effect, as a direct holding that an innocent human being can be defined as a non-person and killed at the discretion of others. The court's opinion was written by Justice Harry Blackmun, but it might as well have been written by Oliver Wendell Holmes, who wrote, "I see no reason for attributing to man a significance different in kind from that which belongs to a baboon or to a grain of sand."[6]

It was inevitable that the Constitution of the United States would degenerate into positivism. The Constitution implicitly recognized a natural law, but its defect was its failure to specify a moral arbiter, external to the state, to interpret the meaning of that higher law in particular situations. Apparently, it was left to the people to decide. But this created a vacuum of authority. If the natural law were to govern and if the people were to determine its meaning, how would the view of the people come to be known? It is not surprising, in view of the Constitution's emphasis on the representative character of government, that government itself moved in to fill the vacuum.

At various stages, Congress, the President, or the Supreme Court has been dominant in determining the meaning of the "higher law" protections recognized by the Constitution. Judge Thomas Cooley described the legislative dominance which prevailed during most of the nineteenth century:

> Except where the constitution has imposed limits upon the legislative power, it must be considered as practically

absolute, whether it accords to natural justice or not in any particular case. The courts are not the guardians of the rights of the people of the State, except as those right are secured by some constitutional provision which comes within the judicial cognizance.[7]

This is positivism, under the rubric of a final legislative determination of the meaning of natural law. Executive supremacy, too, has had its day, especially in the emergencies of the Civil War and both world wars. For example, 70,000 people of Japanese ancestry, including many American citizens, were removed from the West Coast in 1942 and confined in relocation camps. This action, taken pursuant to Presidential authority and with congressional approval, was based on racial criteria. Moreover, the alleged military justification for it was doubtful at best, since the order was not effective until May, 1942, by which time the naval tide in the Pacific had begun to turn against the Japanese. The Supreme Court acquiesced in this extreme measure after giving it a scrutiny that was hardly searching.[8]

Today, the Supreme Court is the sovereign interpreter of the meaning of the constitutional protections, and in a sense, the Supreme Court has become a continuing constitutional convention. In 1868 the Fourteenth Amendment forbade the states to "deprive any person of life, liberty, or property, without due process of law," or to "deny to any person within its jurisdiction the equal protection of the laws." The Supreme Court has interpreted the amendment, particularly its due process clause, to embody various natural rights and principles of fairness in limitation of government power. But the rights, whether the right to make a contract,[9] freedom of association,[10] the right to privacy,[11] or whatever, are protected only because the Court chose to find them in the Fourteenth Amendment or some other part of the Constitution. They are not protected on the ground that they are *above* the Constitution and are binding— whether or not they are found *in* the Constitution. Natural rights are therefore not protected unless they are recognized at least implicitly in the Constitution. It follows that if the Constitution is interpreted by the Supreme Court so as to exclude one of those rights, that exclusion is final unless the Court reverses itself or the Constitution is amended. In *Roe* v. *Wade,* the right to life of the unborn was thus excluded. The Constitution today, in a very real sense, is whatever the judges say it is.

Of course, application by the courts of a higher standard of law would be appropriate only in extreme cases. As a West German court said in 1947, "Whenever the conflict between an enacted law and true justice *reaches unendurable proportions,* the enacted law must yield to justice, and be considered a 'lawless law.'"[12] The Constitution of the United States incorporates certain natural-law principles and these will suffice for the decision of the great majority of cases, without resorting to extraconstitutional principles of justice. But those higher principles of law must be available to the courts and to the people in extreme cases, such as abortion, where the Constitution itself is used to sanction results which are clearly contrary to what the Declaration of Independence called "the laws of Nature and of Nature's God." As Gustav Radbruch said of such laws, "jurists must find the courage to brand them unlawful."[13]

A clear case of positivism was the decision of the New York Court of Appeals, the highest court of that state, in the Byrn case, upholding the permissive 1970 New York abortion law. The court first found as a fact that the unborn child is a human being "upon conception," but it went on to rule that it is up to the legislature to decide which human beings are persons and are therefore entitled to the right to live. For this positivistic proposition the court cited (among others) Hans Kelsen: "What is a legal person is for the law, including, of course, the Constitution, to say, which simply means that upon according legal personality to a thing the law affords it the rights and privileges of a legal person (e.g., Kelsen General Theory of Law and State, pp. 93-109). . . . The point is that it is a policy determination whether legal personality should attach

and not a question of biological or 'natural' correspondence."[14] The Supreme Court, of course, took this same
route in *Roe v. Wade,* where it ruled that whether or not the
unborn child is a human being, he is not a "person" within the meaning of the Fourteenth Amendment.

"By resort to the allegedly vague 'equal protection' and
'due process" clauses," the Supreme Court "has replaced
the choices of the framers by personal predilections of the
Justices."[15] Whether in school busing, legislative apportion-
ment, criminal procedure, or whatever, the popular reaction
is that when the Supreme Court speaks the Constitution
speaks, when in reality the holdings of the court are merely
the result-oriented conclusions of five or more Platonic
guardians who have assumed the power both to revise the
meaning of basic rights and to determine basic policy. The
problem is aggravated because the law has an educative
effect. The edicts of the Supreme Court tend to influence
the popular judgment on morality as well as law.

For example, when Congress in the 1964 Civil Rights
Act forbade racial discrimination in restaurants and other
public accommodations and this law was upheld by the
Court, it had an effect of increasing the general awareness
that it is immoral to hold oneself out as serving the public
and then to refuse service to some because of their race.
On the other hand, the Supreme Court's insulation of
pornography from restraint has contributed to the general
public tolerance of that material. The abortion decisions
have had a similar effect. The result is that while the court
exercises the role of arbiter of the constitutional meaning
of due process and similar concepts, it has come to be the
public instructor on the moral content of the natural law.

It would be a mistake, however, to blame the courts
entirely for the ascendancy of positivism. Instead, the law
tends to reflect the prevailing consensus as well as to shape
it. Today, positivism is characteristic of America's life as
well as its law. The American people, educated to doubt
their capacity to reason to what is right, are subject to
manipulation by politicians and the media. The American

educational system for generations has been pervaded by agnostic pragmatism through the influence of John Dewey (1859-1952) and his followers. Dewey has been well described as "the great protagonist of liberalism, pragmatism, and democracy, in America."[16] As an evolutionist, Dewey regarded man as a mere biological organism, without a spiritual soul. For Dewey, every idea is created by experience. As a pragmatist, he believed that the only test of the truth of an idea is its success in affecting the practical life of society. As William James, another influential pragmatist, said: "The true, to put it very briefly, is only the expedient in the way of our behaving. Expedient in almost any fashion; and expedient in the long run and on the whole of course."[17]

One result of this pragmatism is ethical subjectivism, under which the rightness or wrongness of any action is completely up to the individual:

> The prevalence of the expression "I feel" is a symptom of the softening effect of a pop Deweyism on our students' brains: a lazy acceptance of the view that since nothing is known with assured finality, there are no facts, only opinions, and therefore that one opinion is as good as another.
>
> If we accepted this view with regard to our own disciplines, it would be the death of research, the death of teaching, and the death of our own minds. But our students do accept it with regard to their writing, their literary studies, their aesthetic judgments, and the beliefs they live by. Nothing is true, nothing is false, everything floats, everything is a matter of opinion.[18]

Where pragmatism is the dominant philosophy, positivism will be its form of jurisprudence, for both are essentially the same in their denial that reason can know the truth. In 1974 the Supreme Court declared that "under the First Amendment there is no such thing as a false idea."[19] That statement is, of course, absurd. It means that the idea that there *is* such a thing as a false idea is itself false, thereby contradicting the Court's basic statement. But more importantly, the absurd suspension of judgment as to truth is characteristic of much of American constitutional law. It underlies Justice Holmes' dictum that, "If in the long run the beliefs expressed in proletarian dictatorships are destined to be accepted by the dominant forces of the community, the only meaning of free speech is that they should be given their chance and have their way."[20] It can be seen in the Supreme Court's treatment of religion, contraception, and abortion, as will be discussed in later chapters, and it accounts for much of the court's deference to obscenity and defamatory falsehood.

It would be a waste of time to say to any American court that *Roe* v. *Wade*—or any other decision—is void as contrary to the higher law of God. Thomas Aquinas and Sir Edward Coke would be laughed out of court today. So would George Mason, who said that "all acts of legislature apparently contrary to natural right and justice are, in our laws, and must be in the nature of things, considered as void."[21] Instead, the tone is set by such items as the 1975 report of the United States Commission on Civil Rights on the Constitutional Aspects of the Right to Limit Childbearing. One would think that a civil rights commission would defend the unborn child's civil right to live. Instead, the commission supported the court rulings on positivistic grounds:

> The commission therefore takes no position on the moral or theological debate which surrounds the issue of abortion. Nor does it take a position on whether an individual woman should or should not seek an abortion. The commission's sole position is its affirmation and support of each woman's "constitutional right" as delineated by the Supreme Court.[22]

Or as President John F. Kennedy said in opposing the efforts to overturn the decisions outlawing prayer in public schools: "I think it is important for us, if we are going to maintain our constitutional principles, that we support the

Supreme Court decisions, even though we may not agree with them."[23]

Either the government of the United States is limited by a higher law or it is not. If it is not so limited, it is, of course, positivistic. But if it is so limited, there must be someone, outside the government and the people, to whom it can look for morally binding interpretations of the natural law. Since the natural law is the law of God and since Christ is God, it would be appropriate for that supralegal arbiter of the natural law to be the Vicar of Christ on earth. The power of the Church, said Pope Pius XII, is not limited to "matters strictly religious" but includes "the whole matter of the natural law, its foundation, its interpretation, its application, so far as their moral aspect extends."[24]

I do not mean that the Pope should exercise a veto power over the decisions of the courts or other governmental bodies, or that churchmen should participate in those decisions; rather, what is needed is an external moral interpreter. When the Supreme Court decrees that unborn babies may be killed, objecting citizens ought to be able to point to a source that is accepted by the community as the interpreter of the overriding natural moral law. Otherwise, we are driven to morality by consensus and thence to positivism and agnosticism. When one says the abortion rulings are immoral, another will reply, "That is your private judgment; who is to say?" Contradictory answers cannot both be objectively right. An umpire is needed in the moral sphere, and this has to be the Vicar of Christ. It is the duty of the Church, said the Second Vatican Council, "to give utterance to, and authoritatively to teach, that Truth which is Christ Himself, and also to declare and confirm by her authority those principles of the moral order which have their origin in human nature itself."[25]

If the state, which possesses the power of coercion, is its own interpreter of the natural law, it is not really subject to it at all and the people are at its mercy. And if the state claims to make only legal interpretations, leaving moral questions to the private realm, that in itself is taking a moral position: that law and morality are separated and that the state can act without regard to the moral law. Nor can the majority provide security as an interpreter of the natural law, for someone must decide what is the majority view.

The founders of the American republic tried to make it Christian without the Church. The system worked for a time because the founders, in setting it up, spent the capital they had inherited from pre-Reformation Catholic Christendom. The refusal of the founders to recognize the moral authority of the Vicar of Christ cut the new republic off from the living Christian tradition and ensured that it would draw no further income from that source. The republic was on its own. Private judgment was the rule in matters of religion and morality. And it was to be expected that the state, in the absence of an outside arbiter, would claim the right to exercise its private judgment as to its own conduct.

The point is that no state can remain subject to the natural moral law unless the people freely recognize, and the state affirms, that the higher law is from God and that its custody is in the Vicar of Christ, who is the moral arbiter of that law. This would be a moral recognition, not a technical establishment. It would reconnect the community with the moral treasury of the Church of Christ.

The weakness of the American Constitution vis-a-vis positivism bears out Thomas Babington Macaulay's observation (in another context in 1857) that, "Your Constitution is all sail and no anchor."[26] The ultimate choice is not between public recognition of the moral authority of the Vicar of Christ, on the one hand, and benign toleration on the other. Instead, the choice is between the Church and the total state. If the moral authority of the Pope is not accepted, the state, or the majority, or both, will move in to do the job.

Every society, like every man, has to have a god. There has to be an ultimate authority. If it is not the real God, speaking through his vicar on earth, it will be a god of man's own making. This may be man himself, the consensus, the courts—whatever. Ultimately, in the absence of an external arbiter, that moral authority will center in the state, which already possesses the coercive power. The conflict, then, is between the claim of the Catholic Church and the claim of the total state. It is not surprising, therefore, that the modern totalitarian state sees the Catholic Church as its enemy.

When the Geriatric Welfare Act of 1996 is proposed, you will find the opposition centered in whatever part of the Catholic Church in America that is still united to the Vicar of Christ.

7

The Failure of the Constitution:
Secularism

If we want an innocent target to blame for *Roe* v. *Wade*, we should not overlook Roy Torcaso. When he applied for appointment as a notary public in Maryland, he was refused because the Maryland constitution required that all public officers and employees declare their belief in God, which Torcaso refused to do. In deciding in his favor in 1961, the Supreme Court laid down the principles which made *Roe* v. *Wade* (or something of the sort) inevitable.

In Torcaso's case, the court struck down Maryland's oath requirement because it unconstitutionally invaded the applicant's "freedom of belief and religion" and because the "power and authority of the State of Maryland thus is put on the side of one particular sort of believers—those who are willing to say they believe 'in the existence of God.'"[1] Nontheistic creeds were defined by the court to be religions. The court held that "neither a State nor the Federal Government can constitutionally aid all religions as against non-believers, and neither can aid those religions based on a belief in the existence of God as against those religions founded on different beliefs."[2] In a footnote, Mr.

Justice Black, speaking for the court, said: "Among religions in this country which do not teach what would commonly be considered a belief in the existence of God are Buddhism, Taoism, Ethical Culture, Secular Humanism and others."

When the government of the United States, through the Supreme Court, thus declared its neutrality on the existence of God, the fate of millions of children was sealed. Not that the Supreme Court in the Torcaso case said anything about abortion; it did not have to. By 1961, our public philosophy had become thoroughly positivistic, but a lingering deference to God held matters in check. However, when the state declared its official indifference to God, the dam was breached. Thereafter, the court would treat such issues as abortion only in secular and wholly amoral terms. Under those rules, the unborn child never had a chance.

The relevant clauses of the First Amendment provide that "Congress shall make no law respecting an establishment of religion, or prohibiting the free exercise thereof." The Supreme Court has held that the due-process clause of the Fourteenth Amendment, adopted in 1868, made these restrictions applicable against the states as well as the government of the United States. That clause merely provides that no state may "deprive any person of life, liberty, or property, without due process of law." The claim that this clause was designed to bind a uniform rule on the states in all matters covered by the Bill of Rights is a distortion of the Fourteenth Amendment. It has fastened an artificial uniformity on the states.[3] When the court secularized the First Amendment in the Torcaso case, the mischief was compounded because of the court's edict that its First Amendment rulings are binding on all the states (and local governments) uniformly.

The Constitution of the United States was not intended by its framers to isolate the state from God. When the American Revolution began, there were established, state-supported churches in at least nine colonies. Under these establishments, the established sect (either Anglican or Congregational) alone received public money and official support. Four of these establishments were still in existence when the Constitution was adopted. The establishment clause of the First Amendment was intended to prevent Congress from establishing a national church and, also, from interfering with the existing state establishments. That is why it forbade any law "respecting an establishment of religion."

It is clear that neither the Constitution nor the First Amendment was designed to prohibit the recognition of God by the government of the United States or of any state. The Declaration of Independence acknowledged God in four places. Although the Constitution makes no reference to God, this was because the Constitution is a technical document, and not because of any secularizing purpose. The history of the colonies between 1775 and the Constitutional Convention in 1787 is replete with official acknowledgments of God and supplications for his aid. For example, the Treaty of Paris (with Great Britain at the close of the Revolution in 1783) begins: "In the name of the Most Holy and Undivided Trinity."[4] Pursuant to a resolution of both houses of Congress, an Anglican *Te Deum* service was conducted in St. Paul's Chapel as part of President Washington's first inauguration.[5] And on September 24, 1789, the very day it approved the First Amendment, the Congress called on President Washington to proclaim a national day of thanksgiving and prayer to acknowledge "the many signal favors of Almighty God."[6] President Washington proclaimed the day, and every president (except Thomas Jefferson and Andrew Jackson) has followed his example. If the First Amendment was intended to prevent governmental recognition of the existence of God, was it not strange for Congress to propose that amendment on the same day it called on the president to give thanks to that God whom he was not supposed to acknowledge?

The establishment clause was intended, in the words of Judge Thomas Cooley, to prevent "the setting up or recognition of a state church, or at least the conferring upon one church of special favors and advantages which are denied to others."[7] Mr. Justice Joseph Story, a Unitarian, and a justice on the Supreme Court from 1811 to 1845, spelled out the meaning of the religion clauses of the First Amendment:

> Probably at the time of the adoption of the constitution, and of the first amendment to it . . . the general if not the universal sentiment in America was, that Christianity ought to receive encouragement from the state so far as was not incompatible with the private rights of conscience and the freedom of religious worship. An attempt to level all religions, and to make it a matter of state policy to hold all in utter indifference, would have created universal disapprobation, if not universal indignation.
>
> * * *
>
> The real object of the amendment was not to countenance, much less to advance, Mahometanism, or Judaism, or infidelity, by prostrating Christianity; but to exclude all rivalry among Christian sects, and to prevent any national ecclesiastical establishment which should give to a hierarchy the exclusive patronage of the national government.[8]

In 1892, in *Holy Trinity Church* v. *United States,* the Supreme Court ruled that a federal law forbidding the importation of foreigners under a contract to perform labor could not be construed to apply to a New York church which brought an English minister into the country under a contract to preach. The court recited the legislative history of the act and various religious phrases in American historical documents, and concluded:

> But beyond all these matters no purpose of action against religion can be imputed to any legislation, state or national, because *this is a religious people.* This is historically true. From the discovery of this continent to the present hour, there is a single voice making this affirmation. . . .
> If we pass beyond these matters to a view of American life as expressed by its laws, its business, its customs and its society, we find everywhere a clear recognition of the

same truth. . . . These, and many other matters which might be noticed, add a volume of unofficial declarations to the mass of organic utterances that *this is a Christian nation*. In the face of all these, shall it be believed that a Congress of the United States intended to make it a misdemeanor for a church of this country to contract for the services of a Christian minister residing in another nation?[9]

The establishment clause required that government be neutral among religions, but the critical question is the definition of "religion." In 1890 the Supreme Court declared that "the term 'religion' has reference to one's views of his relations to his Creator, and to the obligations they impose of reverence for his being and character, and of obedience to his will."[10] But in the 1962 and 1963 school prayer cases, the Supreme Court, following Torcaso, changed that definition to include nontheistic as well as theistic creeds and required that government attempt the impossible task of maintaining neutrality between them. In the 1962 school prayer case, *Engel* v. *Vitale*,[11] the Supreme Court ruled that the recitation in public school of a "non-denominational" prayer was unconstitutional, although no pupil was required to participate. The prayer was "Almighty God, we acknowledge our dependence upon Thee, and we beg thy blessings upon us, our parents, our teachers and our country." The next year the Court forbade the devotional recitation of the Lord's Prayer and the reading of the Bible in public schools.[12]

Torcaso v. *Watkins* was probably an interpretation of the free-exercise clause, in that the oath requirement was an infringement of Torcaso's free exercise of his belief. Therefore, it was arguably not a technical interpretation of the establishment clause. But in the 1963 prayer case the Court formally imported the Torcaso definition into the establishment clause. The Court quoted approvingly the dictum from Torcaso that government could not "aid those religions based on a belief in the existence of God as against those religions founded on different beliefs."[13]

Under the original intent of the First Amendment, the free-exercise clause always protected persons of any religion or none. For purposes of free exercise, therefore, "religion" always included nontheistic as well as theistic beliefs. An atheist or agnostic was as fully entitled to the free exercise of his belief as a Baptist. But for purposes of the establishment clause, the original definition of "religion" was more restrictive. The purpose was to require Congress to maintain neutrality among theistic sects while permitting Congress to encourage a belief in generalized Christianity or at least in theism. Neutrality was the mandate of the establishment clause, then as it is today, but the Supreme Court has changed the definition of "religion" to include nontheistic as well as theistic creeds. The neutrality mandate now requires government to maintain neutrality, not among theistic creeds but between theism and nontheism. But this neutrality is impossible. Mr. Justice Brennan, in his concurring opinion in the 1963 prayer case, captured the meaning of that ruling when he argued that the words "under God" could be kept in the pledge of allegiance:

> This general principle might also serve to insulate the various *patriotic* exercises and activities used in the public schools and elsewhere which, whatever may have been their origins, *no longer have a religious purpose or meaning.* The reference to divinity in the revised pledge of allegiance, for example, *may merely recognize the historical fact that our Nation was believed to have been founded "under God."* Thus reciting the pledge may be no more of a religious exercise than the reading aloud of Lincoln's Gettysburg Address, which contains an allusion to the same historical fact.[14]

The words "under God" may therefore be retained in the pledge only if they are merely ceremonial and not to be taken seriously. Thus it would be strictly unconstitutional for the President or a public school teacher to declare *as a fact* that God exists. When the teacher is asked by a pupil whether the Declaration of Independence is true when it says there is a God, he cannot say yes, for that would prefer theism, and he cannot say no, for that would prefer atheism. The only answer he can give is to say that he cannot say one way or the other—that is, that he, in his official capacity in acting for the state, cannot know whether God exists. But that is an implicit preference of the agnostic, nontheistic religion of secular humanism.

In 1965 the federal courts ruled that public school kindergarteners, before they ate their cookies and milk, could not recite, on their own initiative, the Romper Room Grace: "God is Great, God is Good, and we thank Him for our food. Amen." Nor could they recite a grace that said:

> Thank you for the World so Sweet,
> Thank you for the Food we Eat,
> Thank you for the Birds that Sing—
> Thank you, God, for everything.[15]

Two years later a federal court ruled that public school kindergarten children in Illinois could not recite the latter even though they left the word "God" out of the last line. The court's idea was that everyone knows who "you" is— that is, God. The intent is to offer thanks to God, which is unlawful in public schools.[16]

Another court ruled that public high school students could not voluntarily meet in the school gymnasium before school to listen to a volunteer student read the opening "remarks" of the congressional chaplain as contained in the *Congressional Record*. The volunteer reader would "add remarks concerning such subjects as love of neighbor, brotherhood and civic responsibility. At the conclusion of the reading the students are asked to meditate for a short period of time either on the material that has been read or upon anything else they desire." The court held that the congressional chaplain's "remarks" were really prayers and were therefore forbidden in public school. Apparently they are constitutional in Congress because congressmen are less susceptible to "subversion" by religion because they are more mature—a conclusion that is open to some doubt.[17]

Other examples could be cited to show the diligence of the courts in requiring governments at every level to suspend judgment on the existence of God. As a result of such rulings, a generation of public school children has grown to maturity without seeing the state, in the person of their teachers, affirm as a fact that there is a standard of right and wrong that is higher than the state. They have received implicit indoctrination in positivism as well as secularism. However, it would be a mistake to regard this official agnosticism as a purely judicial coup, unrelated to the general erosion of religious conviction. The original plan, under which Congress could promote a generalized Christianity while protecting the free-exercise rights of all, worked as long as the Christian consensus of the American people endured. But as Justice Brennan pointed out in the 1963 prayer case, the religious composition of the American people has changed:

> Our religious composition makes us a vastly more diverse people than were our forefathers. They knew differences chiefly among Protestant sects. Today the Nation is far more heterogeneous religiously, including as it does substantial minorities not only of Catholics and Jews but as well of those who worship no God at all. See *Torcaso* v. *Watkins*, 367 U.S. 488, 495.[18]

The Supreme Court, in adopting secular humanism as the officially established religion, was reflecting as well as promoting a new secular consensus. Without that consensus, the court could not have ruled God out of public institutions. If it had faced a truly Christian people, the court would not have dared to apply the secular creed further in pornography, contraception, abortion, and other matters. Unfortunately, the Christian consensus is gone. And the primary agent in its demise has been the public school.

A strong majority of the American people has consistently

backed the restoration of prayer to the public schools, but this attachment to a symbolic religious observance is largely sentimental. The American public school had become an agency of secularism long before the Supreme Court officially ratified the condition in the school prayer decisions. Public opinion had generally accepted this condition and was in turn influenced by the views of the products of those schools.

The public schools in the beginning were not secular. They were essentially nondenominational Protestant schools. It was in reaction to this condition that Catholic parochial schools were first established. Today, the public schools profess neutrality in religion, but the fact is that no school can be neutral vis-a-vis God. As Patrick Cardinal O'Boyle commented:

> Of course, it may be argued that the public schools need not favor any particular religion or religion at all, for they can proceed on strictly humanistic, pragmatic and secular conceptions. But this is precisely the point. To proceed in this way is itself to establish a religion—secular humanism—and to favor this religion over all others. . . .
>
> Historically, John Dewey, who has so much to do with progressive education, which deeply affected the philosophical foundations of our present public schools, spoke of his own beliefs, which were a form of secular humanism, in religious terms. In a statement first published in 1897, entitled *My Pedagogic Creed,* Dewey said that in shaping children as members of secular society the teacher is "always the prophet of the true God and the usherer in of the kingdom of God."
>
> For Dewey, the true God is not the Holy Trinity, but is the human community; the true kingdom of God is not heaven, but is the secular city perfected by applied science. Dewey claimed that public schools, in contributing to the realization of this ideal, would be doing a genuinely religious work, more so indeed than could be done with all of the paraphernalia of traditional religion.[19]

The public school is a religious institution whose creed

is secularism. This condition would not be cured by working a prayer into the school day or even by allowing instruction by religious groups on public school premises. At best, an amorphous theism would come to be the religion of the public school. In fact, the public schools are not worth saving. Through their "objective" presentation of all points of view they tend to indoctrinate their pupils with agnostic secularism and pragmatism. Through sex education and similar activities, they undermine the family and corrupt the youth by the inculcation of contraceptive and other anti-life attitudes. Whatever parental influence existed in those schools a decade ago has been minimized by the schools' intrusion into the subjects of family life and sex and by the breakup of neighborhood schools under the edicts of federal judges. Overall, the academic quality of the public schools is inferior, as witness the declining Scholastic Aptitude Test (SAT) scores across the nation[20] and the controversy that was generated by the proposal that students who enter the City University of New York must be able to read at an eighth grade level. Increasingly, the public schools are failing to provide even a basic foundation in verbal and mathematical skills. Nine of ten youths in Detroit, seeking to enter the Navy, are rejected because of inability to read and understand the questions on the entrance test.[21]

This is not to say that education can never be a proper function of the state. The Second Vatican Council said it is a function of civil society "to promote the education of youth in many ways, namely to protect the duties and rights of parents and others who share in education and to give them aid; according to the principle of subsidiarity, *when the endeavors of parents and societies are lacking,* to carry out the work of education in accordance with the wishes of the parents; and, moreover, as the common good demands, to build schools and institutions."[22]

Note that, according to the principle of subsidiarity, the state is to carry out the work of education only when "parents and other societies" are unable to do so. Subsidiarity is a practical principle that dictates that public tasks be performed by the lowest possible level of government, and, in the words of Pope Pius XI, "it is wrong to withdraw from the individual and commit to the community at large what private enterprise and endeavor can accomplish."[23] Parents are "the primary and principal educators," and "in a special way, the duty of educating belongs to the Church."[24]

Whatever the theoretical justification for a properly ordered state's conducting schools when parents and churches cannot do it, that justification cannot apply where the state is embarked on the establishment of secular humanism as its national creed. Such a state has no right to educate the young. In this country, moreover, parents and churches, and especially the Catholic Church, are fully capable of educating the youth. And who can doubt that they would be better educated in those schools? The only real difficulty is financial, and it is created by the appetite of the state for taxes to support a public school system which is unnecessary and detrimental.

One widely urged solution is the educational voucher. The state or federal government would give parents a certificate for each child, equivalent to the cost of educating that child in a public school. That voucher could be used at a public school or at any approved private school. The voucher would thus create competition between the public and approved private schools. Also, parental freedom of choice would be enhanced. A tuition tax credit would be similar in its effect; parents could take a credit against their income tax for tuition paid to nonpublic schools.

If the voucher and tax credit were usable at any school requiring the same number of days' attendance as the public schools, they would involve little risk to the independence of those schools. But realistically, as provided in the pending bills in congress, the voucher or tax credit could be applied to tuition only at schools approved by the state. The tension between the state and parents has sharpened in recent years and within the past five years, that tension has become a type of warfare, with state schools claiming competence in moral and behavioral realms that belong to the family. The voucher and the tax credit systems would require that public authorities approve the schools that receive the money. However innocuous that approval might at first appear, the tendency would be for it to become increasingly conditioned on adherence to the substantive standards of the authorities. This clearly is an unacceptable risk. It is hardly likely that the administrators of public education will acquiesce in the growth of truly independent and religious schools under a voucher or tuition tax credit system.

The alternative is to take a stand against public education as such. The impressive growth in recent years of excellent, Bible-oriented Christian schools proves that there is a demand to be filled. Instead of seeking to bolster the public schools by introducing marginal religious instruction, and instead of seeking public aid, it would be better to dig more deeply into our pockets to expand Catholic and other sound Christian schools, to resist public school appropriations as a matter of principle, and to confront public schools on their very right to exist.

What, then, about the proposed constitutional amendment to overturn the school-prayer decisions of the Supreme Court? The effort to obtain that amendment was never properly limited to the schools in its object. The issue is broader, involving the duty of the state to recognize God in all its activities. With respect to the public schools, the remedy is not to infuse a common-denominator religion into them; it is rather to abolish them. It remains important, however, to restore the recognition of God by the state— perhaps by a streamlined prayer amendment that would be relieved of the baggage that could obscure its proper objective and make it a device for the preservation of the public schools. This could be achieved by a constitutional amendment that would simply affirm the truths expressed in the Declaration of Independence and the national motto. It might provide something along these lines:

1. This nation is in fact under God, who has created all
   human beings and endowed them with unalienable rights.
2. Nothing in this Constitution shall prevent the United
   States or any state from affirming this fact.

An amendment of this sort would not be directed specifically to public schools, but it would, incidentally, permit
public school teachers and other public officials to affirm
the existence of God through prayer. The amendment would
be essentially symbolic, but it would put the symbolic issue
squarely in terms of our national affirmations. Either God
is God or the state is god. These are the important things:
the recognition of God by the state and the education of
children by their parents. The public schools are a negative
influence in this entire matter.

In his April 30, 1863, proclamation of a national day of
fast and prayer, President Abraham Lincoln said "it is the
duty of nations as well as of men to own their dependence
upon the overruling power of God . . . and to recognize
the sublime truth, announced in the Holy Scriptures and
proven by all history, that those nations only are blessed
whose God is the Lord."[25] Secularism is now established
as our national creed because, in Lincoln's words, "we
have grown in numbers, wealth and power as no other
nation has ever grown. But we have forgotten God." The
Supreme Court alone has not forgotten God; rather, the
Court reflected the erosion of our belief. As pragmatists
and positivists, we are not sure we can know what is right.
As secularists, we do not know God. It is fitting that our
law should now embody those errors.

8

The Contraceptive Mentality

*For behold, days are coming in which men will say,
"Blessed are the barren, and the wombs that never
bore, and breasts that never nursed" (John 23:29).*

The figures indicate that we are committing race suicide.
In 1957, 35 million American women of childbearing age
produced 4.3 million babies. That was the year of the
highest birth and fertility rates in our history. In 1976,
48 million women of childbearing age produced only 3.2
million babies, our lowest rates ever. There was a slight
temporary upturn in 1977 (what the demographic experts
called a "technical adjustment"), but still the "total fertility
rate," which corresponds roughly to the average completed
family size at current fertility rates, was 1.835 children
per woman of childbearing age—well below the "replacement level" of 2.1 children—at which the population would
ultimately cease to grow. Most demographers attribute this
"irreversible decline in child-bearing" to "the wide availability of cheap, effective contraception, the increasing avail-

ability of abortion, later marriages, easier divorce and
and heightened career aspirations of women."[1]

One result of the declining birth rate is the aging of the
population. The median age of Americans, 29.4 years in
1977, will rise to 35.5 years in 2000 and 38.1 years in
2035. At the same time, the number of children will decline
and the proportion of older people will increase as life
expectancy rises.[2] By 2050, at least one person in every
six in this country will be over 65—double the proportion
for 1950.[3]

For two reasons, the birth decline will not soon be reversed. One is the prevalence of the contraceptive mentality,
which is anti-child. The other is that permanent sterilization
is the most popular form of contraception.

The risks involved in the contraceptive pill are a main
cause of the popularity of sterilization, especially among
women. A 1977 British study, for example, concluded that
pill users in general face a 40 percent higher death rate
than women the same age who have never used the pill.[4]
In the late 1960s in this country, vasectomy, or sterilization
of the male, was the most common form of sterilization.
Female sterilization was much more complicated. But easier
methods of tubal ligation brought a sharp increase in female
sterilizations after 1970. They now account for more than half
of the sterilizations performed each year.[5] In 1975, 75 percent of married couples of childbearing age in this country
were using some form of contraception.[6] In 1973, in at
least one in every four couples using contraception, one or
both spouses had been sterilized. By 1977 the figure had
risen to one in three.[7] Worldwide, one of every ten couples
of childbearing age relies on sterilization.[8]

In the past few years in this country there has been a
sharp rise in hysterectomies, in which the womb is removed.
There were 750,000 hysterectomies in 1975, compared to
685,000 tonsillectomies, once the most prevalent major
surgery. The number of hysterectomies is second only to
abortions in this country.[9] The Department of Health,
Education, and Welfare announced in December 1977 that

it would no longer pay for hysterectomies performed solely for contraceptive reasons.[10] But this restriction will have only marginal impact, and it cannot replace the wombs already removed. Hysterectomy is obviously permanent. But in practical terms, so is every other type of sterilization. New surgical techniques may increase the possibility of reversal for males and females, but the researchers who developed these techniques emphasize the slim prospects of reversal and warn that neither men nor women should seek sterilization unless they intend it to be permanent.[11]

The Catholic Church has always taught that all forms of contraception, including contraceptive sterilization, are objectively wrong. Indeed, until the Anglican Lambeth Conference of 1930, all major Christian denominations taught the wrongness of contraception. The evil of contraception is not merely a matter of Church discipline, like meatless Fridays. It is rooted in the nature of man.

As in all such matters, however, it is important to distinguish between objective wrong and subjective culpability. Whether one who commits an objective wrong is subjectively culpable will depend on the state of his knowledge and the consent of his will. "Conscience" is the capacity of man to judge the moral rightness or wrongness of a particular act. First, one is obliged to follow the judgment of his conscience if it is clear, even if it is objectively in error. (If one's conscience is in error, one may be culpable for having failed to form it correctly, but one should follow it.) Second, one may never act on a doubtful conscience. If one is in doubt about the morality of an act, he should take the safer course and refrain from performing that act. What is often overlooked, however, is the duty to form one's conscience correctly. One should seek information and pray for guidance in forming his conscience. Catholics are obliged to give "religious submission of will and of mind" to the authentic teachings of the pope, as in *Humanae Vitae,* even when they are not formally infallible pronouncements.[12] Whether a person is subjectively culpable for performing an objectively wrong act is a matter for God and the confessor.

Our discussion of contraception, as of other evils, is confined to the objective order and does not imply any judgment as to the subjective culpability, or lack of it, of particular persons.[13]

Contraception is the separation of love from life. It is the willful separation of the unitive and procreative aspects of the sexual act, where God ordained that they be intrinsically united. Pope Paul VI, in his 1968 encyclical *Humanae Vitae,* taught that

> each and every marriage act (*quilibet matrimonii usus*) must remain open to the transmission of life.
>
> That teaching, often set forth by the magisterium, is founded upon the inseparable connection, willed by God and unable to be broken by man on his own initiative, between the two meanings of the conjugal act: the unitive meaning and the procreative meaning. Indeed, by its intimate structure, the conjugal act, while most closely uniting husband and wife, capacitates them for the generation of new lives, according to laws inscribed in the very being of man and of woman. By safeguarding both these essential aspects, the unitive and the procreative, the conjugal act preserves in its fullness the sense of true mutual love and its ordination toward man's most high calling to parenthood.
>
> Equally to be excluded, as the teaching authority of the Church has frequently declared, is direct sterilization, whether perpetual or temporary, whether of the man or of the woman. Similarly excluded is every action which, either in anticipation of the conjugal act, or in its accomplishment, or in the development of its natural consequences, proposes, whether as an end or as a means, to render procreation impossible.

Contraceptionists criticize the Catholic teaching because it permits partial abstinence as a method of avoiding pregnancy. (However, there must be a serious reason for practicing partial abstinence for that purpose.) The critics say there is no difference between contraception and partial abstinence and they accuse the Church of hypocrisy on that point. But in fact there is a great difference, as Pope Paul pointed out:

> The Church is coherent with herself when she considers recourse to the infecund periods to be licit, while at the same time condemning, as being always illicit, the use of means directly contrary to fecundation, even if such use is inspired by reasons which may appear honest and serious. In reality, there are essential differences between the two cases; in the former, the married couple make legitimate use of a natural disposition; in the latter, they impede the development of natural processes. It is true that, in the one and the other case, the married couple are concordant in the positive will of avoiding children for plausible reasons, seeking the certainty that the offspring will not arrive; but it is also true that only in the former case are they able to renounce the use of marriage in the fecund periods when, for just motives, procreation is not desirable, while making use of it during infecund periods to manifest their affection and to safeguard their mutual fidelity. By so doing, they give proof of a truly and integrally honest love.[14]

To appreciate the distinction, we should separate the two periods: the fertile period, during which abstinence is practiced, and the infertile period, during which relations are had. During the fertile period, the abstaining couple does nothing. This is wrong only if there is a duty to have sex relations during a given time; but there is no such duty. The parties are merely refraining, for a serious reason, from the exercise of an act which it is their privilege, but not their duty, to perform. On the other hand, the parties act during the infertile period. And they do so in the way that nature ordains, accepting the intrinsic relation between sex and babies and doing nothing to inhibit the natural tendency of the act toward that end. True, they may have a desire not to have children, but they are willing to accept whatever happens in the natural performance of the act. One need not have a specific intent to have a child every time one has relations. And whatever their personal wishes, they do nothing to frustrate the natural tendency of that particular act.

Now consider the contracepting couple. They perform the act when they want to perform it, but they take artificial preventive measures. They say to God, "We want to use this privilege, this gift you gave us, but we want only part of it. We want the recreational. You keep the procreational." The irony is that their contraceptive precautions, their drugs and plugs, are for the purpose of enhancing the unitive aspect of sex, but in willfully rendering it barren, they destroy even its unitive character. The union of husband and wife should be a mutual self-donation, but with contraception there is a holding back. There is a lack of trust in God—and, before long, in each other. For the contraceptive sexual act is an essay in self-gratification, however much the rhetoric of "caring" might be used. Contraception reduces the act to an exercise in mutual masturbation.

Contraception is the characteristic irresponsibility of our day. On the other hand, the newer methods of natural family planning, including the Billings method (developed by Doctors John and Lyn Billings), are wholly effective and consistent with the teaching of the Church.[15] The Church in the United States is promoting the legitimate use of natural family planning, which requires abstinence for a few days each month. Mrs. Nordis Christenson, a Protestant, described her reasons for rejecting contraception and choosing natural family planning:

> We know contraception prevents conception. It is much easier to see that, than to ascertain what else it does. Could this be a contributing factor to the immature, unsatisfying sex life which marriage counselors hear about and divorce statistics confirm? Is contraception an unsuspected blight on modern marriage?
>
> What are we saying to ourselves psychologically, when we prepare for this most intimate act by donning contraceptive machinery, or by negating the act chemically? Can we treat ourselves like a machine, close off an undesirable valve and expect the rest of the machine to operate without difficulty? As persons we are a profound

union of many components which are subtly interrelated and interdependent. We are much more than a rational machine. Fr. Charles Curran, noted Catholic moral theologian who led the theological opposition to Pope Paul's encyclical forbidding the use of contraception, criticizes the Pope for too simplistic and physical a view of intercourse. But this is precisely the argument against contraception: the use of contraceptives presupposes that a mere physical interruption of conception is all that takes place. Otherwise, we think, nothing is affected; the psychology of sex, the intimate relationship, the marriage itself are untouched. Is not *this* a too-simplistic view of human nature and the sex act? . . .

It's time to consider again the value of self-denial. It has been the witness of saints through the ages that self-denial, by the grace of God, doesn't impoverish but rather enriches us. This has been our experience. Periods of sexual abstinance refresh and renew the relationship.[16]

Contraception is widely advanced as an alternative to abortion, but even in materialistic and pragmatic terms, contraception is not the remedy. Instead, it adds to the abortion problem. Widespread contraception tends to require abortion as a "backstop." And if abortion is readily available, people tend to be reluctant to bother with contraception. The two evils feed on one another. But apart from this, there is an intrinsic reason why contraception can never be the "solution" to abortion. Contraception is the prevention of life while abortion is the taking of life. However, both come from a common root: separation of the unitive and the procreative aspects of sex. The contraceptive mentality of not wanting babies tends to reduce the objection to abortion to the emotional or esthetic. The contraceptive mentality is hedonistic, regarding comfort, worldly success, and pleasure as the primary aims of life. It is not surprising that the claim of an inconvenient unborn and, therefore, unseen child does not fare well against that mentality.

Another important link between contraception and abortion is technological. The "morning after" pill is abortifacient, yet it is commonly promoted as a contraceptive. Intrauterine devices evidently operate as an abortifacient by preventing implantation of the blastocyst, the fertilized ovum, in the wall of the womb. A common misrepresentation is that the intrauterine device is a contraceptive. Dr. Elizabeth B. Connell, associate director for Health Sciences of the Rockefeller Foundation, describes it as (after the pill) "the next most commonly used form of medical contraception."[17]

The Worcester Foundation for Experimental Biology, at Clark University in Massachusetts, helped to develop the contraceptive pill in 1956. Now the foundation is developing a do-it-yourself home abortion kit, involving the self-administration of vaginal suppositories that contain prostaglandins. This method would induce early abortion, preferably during the first month and, it is hoped, with fewer side effects than other methods.[18] The Worcester research is only one of many research projects along these lines. The Food and Drug Administration has approved a prostaglandin suppository for "midtrimester" use that is 97 percent effective. It was described by the director of the Office of Population of the Agency for International Development as the "ultimate contraceptive." It is, however, an abortifacient.[19]

Early-abortion pills and similar techniques allow a woman to rid herself of a possible pregnancy without being sure that she was pregnant. Whether by "menstrual extraction," a "morning after" pill, a "once-a-month" pill, a suppository, or whatever, the abortion of the future will be done by pills and chemicals that are promoted as contraceptives. Surgical abortions, as we know them, will be less and less important. If we concentrate on the prohibition of surgical abortion and advance contraception as a desired alternative, we will find that we have been outflanked and that massive abortion will have been institutionalized under the pretext of contraception. Coherent opposition to abortion, therefore, requires equally strong opposition to contraception and to the contraceptive mentality.

The contraceptive ethic, because it denies that life is always good, prepared the ground for permissive abortion. Once abortion had accustomed people to the idea that burdensome lives are not worth living, the way was clear for euthanasia as a "cure" for the aged and the "useless." Like abortion and euthanasia, contraception was a direct result of positivism and secularism. If, through positivism, we liberate ourself from objective morality and if, as a secularist, we don't care about life after death, we will apply those attitudes to escape the most basic and burdensome responsibilities—the proper use of sex, the raising of children, and the care of the helpless. The result is a cheapening of life at every stage. When technology presented us with the pill, we were too debased to see it for what it is and to reject it. Indeed, intensified research into the pill in the 1950s was a symptom of the decadence that was far advanced and lacked only the technical means for its indulgence. Now, in every age bracket the contraceptive ethic prevails. The popularity of sterilization is another measure of our decline. A generation of aging adolescents must have its toys, and will not be deprived. So necessary to them is unrestricted coupling that females submit to the risk of the pill. Or as a tradeoff, to escape the hazards of the pill and the possibility of a baby, the male will be altered or the female will be spayed, or both.

One characteristic of contraception is its tendency to depersonalize the woman. Pope Paul, in *Humanae Vitae,* warned that contraception would cause women to be viewed as sex objects, that "man, growing used to the employment of anti-conceptive practices, may finally lose respect for the woman and, no longer caring for her physical and psychological equilibrium, may come to the point of considering her as a mere instrument of selfish enjoyment, and no longer as his respected and beloved companion."

This depersonalization of a human being is the principle of the Supreme Court's abortion rulings. It is also the essence of pornography, where the woman is an object of utility. George Kennan, a former United States ambassador to the Soviet Union, wrote that the "general decadence of Western European society" is evidenced by the inability of Western countries to "put an end to the pornographic invasion that has overcome them."[20] It is difficult to see how a contraceptive society could be anything but tolerant toward pornography, because pornography, like contraception, is the separation of sex from life and the reduction of sex to an exercise in self-gratification.

The "legitimization" of homosexual activity is also predictable in a contraceptive society, which cannot say that homosexual relations are objectively wrong without condemning itself. Instead, homosexual living must be regarded as an "alternate" life style—which is what it is, if sex has no inherent relation to reproduction.

Homosexual activity is a dramatic example of the separation of the unitive and procreative aspects of sex. The public schools of San Francisco (where it is estimated that 100,000 of the city's 680,000 residents are homosexual) have added a course on homosexual life styles to the curriculum. Superintendent Robert Alioto called it "just an adjustment of curriculum to reflect San Francisco's social composition and family lifestyles." He said San Francisco is in "the forefront in attempting to reduce and eliminate discrimination for minorities and for people who have alternate lifestyles."[21]

The Congregation for the Doctrine of the Faith, in its Declaration on Certain Questions concerning Sexual Ethics, approved by Pope Paul and issued on December 29, 1975, condemned homosexual relations as always objectively wrong:

> For according to the objective moral order, homosexual relations are acts which lack an essential and indispensable finality. In Sacred Scripture they are condemned as a serious depravity and even presented as the sad consequence of rejecting God. This judgment of Scripture does not of course permit us to conclude that all those who suffer from this anomaly are personally responsible for it, but it does attest to the fact that homosexual acts are intrinsically disordered and can in no case be approved of.

The point is that legalization and social approval of homosexual activity are inevitable in a society which is positivistic, denying objective moral norms; which is secular, denying God; and which is contraceptive, denying the intrinsic relation of love to life.

Much concern is voiced over teenage promiscuity. Alfred F. Moran, vice president of Planned Parenthood of New York City, claims that "teenage sexuality has become the most critical epidemic problem facing the country." [22] Yet his answer, predictably, is more sex education and more birth control, including abortion. Although birth and fertility rates in the nation fell to a new low in 1975, the only increase was for girls aged 10 through 14, who accounted for 12,624 births, four-tenths of 1 percent of all births that year. [23]

Teen-age promiscuity should not be surprising in a contraceptive society. In addition to the inducements provided by imprudent sex education, the media, and the availability of contraception and abortion, part of the problem is due to parental example. One does not have to be a Rhodes scholar to know that sex inherently has something to do with babies. That is why, according to the natural moral law and the Commandments, sex is properly reserved for marriage, because the natural way to raise children is in a monogamous, lifetime marriage. But if children see their parents, in their practice of contraception, behave as if sex has no inherent relationship to reproduction, it should not be surprising that those children draw the conclusion that sex does not have to be reserved for marriage.

Indeed, it is fair to say that the increase in divorce is also influenced by the contraceptive mentality. In 1976 there were 2,133,000 marriages and 1,077,000 divorces—one divorce for every two marriages, and more than twice the rate in 1966. [24] The rate of increase in the divorce rate may be tapering off but little substantial improvement is in sight. The divorce rate soared during the years in which contraception became practically universal and sterilization became the most popular method. If sex and marriage are not intrinsically related to life, then marriage loses its reason for permanence. It tends to become an alliance for individual self-fulfillment—what Pope Paul called "the juxtaposition of two solitudes."[25] The refusal to accept responsibility for others and to endure frustration is characteristic of the contraceptive mind. According to Dr. Edward Lenoski, director of pediatric emergency services at Los Angeles County Hospital, 90 percent of the battered children in a six-year study "were planned pregnancies."[26] Since the introduction of the pill, child beating has increased threefold.

The disintegration of the family is reflected in American law which in turn accelerates that disintegration. Apart from the rapidly growing adoption of no-fault divorce laws, the decisions of the Supreme Court reflect an atomistic view of the family that is hostile to the Christian tradition, although there was a time when the Supreme Court explicitly defended the Christian family. In 1890, Justice Joseph P. Bradley condemned polygamy as "contrary to the spirit of Christianity and of the civilization which Christianity has produced in the Western world."[27] In 1925, the Supreme Court held unconstitutional an Oregon statute that would have abolished parochial and other private schools by requiring all children to attend public schools. "The child is not the mere creature of the state; those who nurture him and direct his destiny," said the Court, "have the right, coupled with the high duty, to recognize and prepare him for additional obligations."[28]

In 1965, however, in *Griswold* v. *Connecticut,*[29] the Court discovered a constitutional right of privacy in the "penumbras formed by emanations from the Bill of Rights", whatever that means. The Griswold decision invalidated a Connecticut law forbidding the use of contraceptives by married couples, as well as the distribution of such items. (That law did involve an invasion of marital privacy. How else would the state get its evidence?) The principle, however, was soon extended beyond marital privacy and beyond the prohibition of the *use* of contraceptives. In *Eisenstadt* v. *Baird*[30] in 1972, the Court reversed the Massachusetts conviction of William Baird for distributing contraceptives to unmarried persons, holding that "whatever the rights of the individual to access to contraceptives may be, the rights must be the same for the unmarried and the married alike." The "marital couple," said the Court, "is not an independent entity with a mind and heart of its own, but an association of two individuals each with a separate intellectual and emotional makeup. If the right of privacy means anything, it is the right of the *individual,* married or single, to be free from unwarranted governmental intrusion into matters so fundamentally affecting a person as the decision whether to bear or beget a child" (emphasis in original).

The Court thus reduces marriage to a mere personal contract, and the family is no longer treated as "the natural, primary cell of human society."[31] The marriage contract is only a contract, just as an agreement by one person to cut another's lawn every week is a contract. If both parties decide to terminate the lawn-cutting arrangement, or if only one wants out, the law will not compel them to continue in it. So if one spouse, or both, wants to terminate the family relation, the law will not interfere. No-fault divorce is the logical outcome of this atomization of the family.

The process continued in *Planned Parenthood* v. *Danforth,*[32] where the Supreme Court ruled that a state may not require parental consent for an abortion on an unmarried woman under 18; nor could the consent of a married woman's husband be required before she killed their child by abortion. In *Carey* v. *Population Services International*[33] the Court struck down a New York law which prohibited distribution of contraceptives to anyone under 16, forbade distribution of contraceptives to anyone over 16 by anyone other than a licensed pharmacist, and banned the advertising and display of contraceptives. In holding this law unconstitutional, the Court applied to young children "the constitutional protection of individual autonomy in matters of childbearing." Those children, therefore, may obtain their contraceptives, as well as abortions, from Planned Parenthood without parental consent, and they may buy contraceptives by mail and perhaps even from vending machines in subways.

Also in 1977, the Court struck down an East Cleveland housing ordinance which limited occupancy to a single family and which defined "family" so as to exclude the extended family (cousins, etc.). This decision is sound on the limited facts of that case, but the Court said: "Our decisions establish that the Constitution protects the sanctity of the family precisely because the institution of the family is deeply rooted in this nation's history and tradition."[34] The Court recognized the family not for Justice Bradley's reason in 1890, that the family is essential to the "spirit of Christianity"[35]; instead, the family is protected because it is part of "this nation's history and tradition," which of course are defined by the Supreme Court itself. This is positivism, leaving the protection of the family to the Supreme Court, unrestrained by any higher standard. In the most important areas of reproduction and parental control of children, the Supreme Court interprets history and tradition so as to atomize the family and destroy its integrity.

The nature of the positivist, secular state requires that it be hostile to the family and to all independent societies between it and the people whom is must control. In 1789, when the French revolutionary intellectuals found the National Assembly at their disposal, one of their early actions was to dissolve all trade guilds, corporations, and unions.[36] A Soviet decree in August 1918 deprived all religious organizations of their character as religious persons.[37] The hostility of both revolutions to the family needs no elaboration. The total state can tolerate no truly independent groups that compete for the loyalty of its subjects. Achievement of this aim of the state is facilitated in a contraceptive society. Self-indulgent and permissive, such a society invites repression to curb its own indiscipline.

The contraceptive mind tends to be hostile to new or burdensome life. Thus it is not surprising when that attitude is applied to the child in the womb, or to his grandmother, and when it is raised to the level of state policy. The only remedy for this is a widespread conviction that life is a gift of God and that it is good.

9

Abortion: The Problem

The lady bid $30. She was the highest bidder and won—an abortion, normally priced at $150—at the Delta Women's Clinic.[1] The auction, a fund-raising enterprise of the Louisiana branch of the American Civil Liberties Union, calls to mind the slave auctions so rhetorically opposed by the ACLU in other situations. Nor was this unknown child the only innocent whose life was priced at thirty pieces of silver.

Every year about 1.2 million American babies are legally killed by abortion. Our battle deaths in all the wars this nation ever fought, from the Revolution through Vietnam, totaled about 669,000.[2] The body count of unborn babies reaches that figure about every seven months. Every year abortion wipes out the equivalent of the population of Houston or the combined populations of Kansas City, Minneapolis, and Miami. There are more abortions than live births in New York City and Washington, D.C.[3] One-third of the abortions in this country are performed on teen-agers, and more girls 14 and under had abortions than delivered children in 1977.[4] There are more abortions than any other operation in this country. Tonsillectomies used to be first, but they are fading fast in third, with hysterectomies in second place.

There are between 30 million and 55 million abortions in the world each year—at least one for every four births—and there is a booming international black market in babies for adoption.[5]

There is no doubt that every abortion, at whatever stage of pregnancy, kills a living human being. A child's life begins at fertilization, the joinder of the male sperm and the female ovum. At 18 days after conception the unborn child's heart starts to beat. When he weighs 1/30th of an ounce, at 6 weeks, he has every internal organ he will have as an adult. He has a mouth, lips, tongue, and twenty buds for his milk teeth. His primitive skeletal system is developed by this time. At 43 days his brain waves can be detected by electroencephalogram. The absence of such brain waves is one of the modern indicators of death; their presence indicates life. But this does not mean that life begins at 43 days. The brain is apparently the last activity to go at death but it is not the first to come when human life begins. Also at 6 weeks, the unborn child has recognizable fingers, knees, ankles, and toes. If you stroke his lips, he will bend his body to one side and make a quick, backward motion with his arms. This is a "total pattern response," in that it involves most of his body rather than one part. At 8 weeks, his brain is fully present, his stomach secretes gastric juices, and if you tickle his nose he will flex his head backward away from the stimulus. At 9 weeks, electrocardiogram recordings of his heart can be taken, and he squints, swallows, and moves his tongue. If you stroke his palm, he will make a tight fist. At 11 weeks he has fingernails, all his body systems are working, and he sucks his thumb. He has spontaneous movement without stimulation. He breathes fluid steadily, getting oxygen through the umbilical cord. At 10 weeks he feels pain. At 12 weeks he will kick his legs, turn his feet and fan his toes, bend his wrists, turn his head, squint, frown, open his mouth, and press his lips tightly together. At 16 weeks he has eyelashes and at 18 weeks he cries, although we hear no sound because there is no air in the womb. At 20 weeks he will react to loud noises and his mother's voice. If he is given an intrauterine transfusion, frequently two people have to do it: one to hold him, to keep him from jumping away from the needle, and the other to make the injection.[6]

The new science of fetology is aimed at the care of the unborn child while he is still in the womb.[7] The Declaration of Geneva, a medical vow adopted by the General Assembly of the World Medical Associations in 1948 and 1968, includes a doctor's oath to be taken at the time of admission as a member of the medical profession: "I will maintain the utmost respect for human life, from the time of conception."

When permissive abortion was proposed in the mid-1960s it was argued that nobody knows when life begins, but this confused the opposition only for a while. Science has long known that "it is the penetration of the ovum by a spermatozoon and the resultant mingling of the nuclear material each brings to the union that constitutes the culmination of the process of *fertilization* and marks the initiation of the life of a new individual."[8] The next argument was that even if life is present at conception, it is not human life. The problem with this, of course, is that the living product of human parents *has* to be human. What else could it be— a giraffe, a doorknob? Never was it known that two individuals of one species generated an offspring of a different species. Or could an apple tree produce roses?

In March of 1977, CBS–TV showed the film *The Miracle Months* on prime time. Using medical optical technologies such as thermography, cinemicrography, and fiberoscopy, the film showed closeups of the unborn child a few days after fertilization and throughout gestation until birth. "The visuals of what goes on inside the body," said the medical director of the program, "give man a chance to see himself all over again."[9] In this and other ways, the public saw through the deceptive arguments that there is no new life at conception or that it is not human life. Consequently, the proponents of abortion have shifted ground.

On one hand, they argue, as we saw in chapter 8, that conception is an extended process which is not complete until after implantation in the womb. Therefore, they argue, intrauterine devices and other early abortifacients are really contraceptives. On the other hand, abortion advocates are now urging that, even conceding that human life is present at fertilization, it is better for that life to be "terminated" rather than live unwanted, deprived, defective, etc. This is the process of depersonalization, in line with the view of the Supreme Court that, whether or not the unborn child is a human being, he is not a person and therefore is not entitled to the right to live. In the Court's view, permissive abortion is a vindication of the mother's right to privacy. But as we shall see in chapter 10, abortion seems now to be, not the right to terminate a pregnancy, but the right to kill one's baby even if he could survive the termination of the pregnancy.

The Upjohn Company markets a prostaglandin, Prostin E^2 vaginal suppositories for the elective termination of pregnancy from and after the 12th week of gestation. But, "Unlike the use of 20% hypertonic saline which usually has a lethal effect on the fetus, the administration of Prostin E^2 vaginal suppositories does not appear to directly affect the integrity of the feto-placental unit and there exists a possibility that a live-born fetus may occur, particularly as gestational age approaches the end of the second trimester." But in an abortion the objective is to kill a baby. "Therefore," the Upjohn information sheet continues, "any failed pregnancy termination with Prostin E^2 should be completed by some other means."[10] The baby who survives the first attempt on his life should be drowned, smothered—anything—to get rid of him.

The depersonalization of the unborn child is also evident in the widespread use of aborted children for research and experimental purposes. The consent of the person who is experimented upon is a basic requirement where such experiments are conducted for the benefit of others or of mankind in general, according to the Nuremberg rules that were developed from the trials of German doctors after World War II and the 1964 Helsinki Declaration of the World Medical Association. Where experiments are conducted on a baby in the womb who is slated for abortion, the inability to get his consent is obvious. And the mother, clearly, is disqualified from consenting on behalf of the child whom she chooses to kill. There is no essential difference between experimenting on a child in the womb who is intended to be aborted, whether or not he is viable, and experimenting without their consent on the adult dying, the incompetent, and even criminals who have been condemned to death. Where an experiment is conducted on a living baby after he is aborted, there is, again, an obvious lack of consent. But even an experiment on the dead body of an abortion victim should be prohibited.

It cannot be said that an experiment on a cadaver becomes intrinsically immoral because the subject met his death as the result of a wrongful act by another person. It is not inherently wrong, therefore, to experiment on the corpse of a murder victim, provided the necessary consent is obtained from the proper custodian of the body. The lack of proper consent, of course, is an obstacle to experimentation on the corpse of an abortion victim. But even apart from the consent issue, there is a compelling reason why such experiments should not be permitted. Even though an experiment is not intrinsically wrong because the subject met his death by murder, experiments on abortion victims are indefensible because of extrinsic circumstances. Those circumstances include the overall abortion climate: the fact that abortion is a "growth industry" and that experimentation is a promotion of that industry because it uses its by-products, that is, bodies, and lends respectability to the entire industry. In proper context, those who experiment on aborted bodies are part of the abortion industry. The claimed utility of the experiments is no excuse, just as the utility of lampshades was no excuse for those who obtained them with knowledge that they were made from the skin of victims of Nazi gas chambers. Where a baby has been intentionally aborted, or is intended to be aborted, all experiments on him should be prohibited, whatever the prospect of gaining useful information from such experiments.

Before Colorado and California enacted the first "liberalized" American abortion laws in 1967, the law of every state permitted abortion where it was necessary to save the life of the mother. This allowance, adopted in the nineteenth century before science was sure of what went on inside the womb, was an exception to the general common-law rule that one is not allowed to kill an innocent nonaggressor even to save his own life. (If two men are on a one-man life raft, neither has the right to throw the other overboard;[11] otherwise, might would make right.) Today, the termination of a pregnancy may be necessary to save the mother's life only in such cases as the ectopic pregnancy (where the fertilized ovum begins to grow in the fallopian tube) and the cancerous womb. If the ectopic pregnancy is not removed, the mother will be likely to die. Catholic teaching permits the removal of the damaged portion of the tube, including the developing human being, when there is clear and imminent danger to the mother's life. And if the cancer of the womb is such that the only way to save the mother's life is to remove the womb, with the baby inside, and the operation cannot be delayed until the baby is viable, the womb may properly be removed, even though it results in the unintended death of the child.

The Ethical and Religious Directives for Catholic Health Facilities, issued by the National Conference of Catholic Bishops in 1971, specified that

in extrauterine pregnancy the dangerously affected part of the mother (e.g., cervix, ovary, or fallopian tube) may be removed, even though fetal death is foreseen, provided that: *a.* the affected part is presumed already to be so damaged and dangerously affected as to warrant its removal; and

that *b.* the operation is not just a separation of the embryo
or fetus from its site within the part (which would be a
direct abortion from a uterine appendage); and that *c.* the
operation cannot be postponed without notably increasing
the danger to the mother.[12]

In moral terms, these operations are justified by the
principle of the double effect, which requires that the
following conditions be met:

1. The action (removal of the diseased womb) is good; it
   consists in excising an infected part of the human
   body.
2. The good effect (saving the mother's life) is not obtained by means of the evil effect (death of the fetus).
   It would be just the opposite, e.g., if the fetus were
   killed in order to save the reputation of an unwed
   mother.
3. There is sufficient reason for permitting the unsought
   evil effect that unavoidably follows. Here the Church's
   guidance is essential in judging that there is sufficient
   reason.
4. The evil effect is not intended in itself, but is merely
   allowed as a necessary consequence of the good effect.

Summarily, then, the womb belongs to the mother just as
completely after a pregnancy as before. If she were not
pregnant, she would clearly be justified to save her life
by removing a diseased organ that was threatening her life.
The presence of the fetus does not deprive her of this
fundamental right.[13]

Such an operation, therefore, when performed under the
necessary conditions, is not the direct abortion (i.e., the in-
tentional killing of the child to achieve some other end),
which the moral law forbids. In the eyes of the civil law,
such operations are not abortions at all, within the terms
of any legal prohibition of abortion. A prosecution has
never even been attempted, let alone successfully concluded,
where such an operation was at issue—whether or not
the mother's life was at stake. Therefore, it is not neces-

sary to provide specifically for these operations as an exception to a legal ban against abortion. They are not within the contemplation of any legal prohibition of abortion and would therefore not be forbidden even if the law were to ban all abortions in the legal sense of the term. The advocates of abortion would never be satisfied with a law which permits abortions only to save the life of the mother. Their objective has always been completely permissive abortion, which they have now achieved. In the 1960s, however, they cloaked their design and argued only for certain exceptions, such as the allowance of abortion where the child was conceived by rape or incest, or where he would likely be defective, or where the mother's mental or physical health would be impaired by continuation of the pregnancy.

The rape and incest arguments were used to attract emotional support for abortion, despite the fact that pregnancy as a result of rape is extremely rare. The stress of the rape situation operates to inhibit conception. And even under Catholic teaching, measures may be taken, up to the time when conception must be presumed to have occurred, to prevent the joinder of the sperm and the ovum. But once that joinder occurs, a new human life is in being.[14] The woman has the right to resist the aggressor and his sperm, but the innocent child is not an agressor. The solution to pregnancy by rape is not the negative one of killing. It is the provision of adequate financial, social, and medical help to women in that predicament and it is more effective prosecution and confinement of rapists. The argument from incest is even less plausible than the argument from rape. Incest is a voluntary act on the woman's part; otherwise it would be rape. And to kill the child because of the identity of his father is hardly fair. Here again the positive solution of support should be pursued.

Another reason that has been advanced for abortion is the risk that the child would be defective. Today, some genetic birth defects can be detected in the womb, and Dr James R. Sorenson of Boston University School of

Medicine has predicted that it might soon become "cultural-ly acceptable and even expected to avoid the birth of a defective child."[15] But to kill the unborn child because he is defective is exactly what the Nazis did to Jews, Gypsies, and other "inferior" minorities whose lives were "not worth living" and who were killed "for their own good." There is an echo of Jeremy Bentham and hedonism here, where the only values are pleasure and pain. If the child, or the senile aged, cannot experience what we regard as a suf-ficient amount of pleasure, we regard his life as worthless and him as a non-person.

Abortion is also advocated where it would promote the physical or mental health of the mother, even though her life is not threatened by the pregnancy. In no other situa-tion does the law permit you to kill an innocent nonag-gressor because he impairs your health. Abortion for the mother's health is a euphemism for elective abortion, par-ticularly with reference to mental health. In fact, numerous studies show that abortion is dangerous to the physical health of the mother[16] and often causes psychological after effects of guilt and longing for her dead child. "Jane Doe," writing in the New York *Times,* described her abortion and concluded:

> It certainly does make more sense not to be having a baby right now—we say that to each other all the time. But I have this ghost now. A very little ghost that only appears when I'm seeing something beautiful, like the full moon on the ocean last weekend. And the baby waves at me. And I wave at the baby. "Of course, we have room," I cry to the ghost. "Of course, we do."[17]

It is still argued that legalized abortion is necessary be-cause women "are going to have abortions anyway" and it is better to have them legalized and safe rather than force them to resort to "back alley" abortionists. The proponents claim that thousands of women were dying at the hands of illegal abortionists before liberalization, which began in Colorado and California in 1967. But in 1966 there

were 1,049 maternal deaths from all causes in this country
and there were 189 maternal abortion deaths, according to
the National Center for Health Statistics of the Department
of Health, Education, and Welfare.[18] The relative figures
are comparable for the preceding years and for the years
after legalization. Moreover, as Dr. Thomas Hilgers of St.
Louis University School of Medicine said, the comparison
of abortion-related maternal mortality rates with maternal
mortality rates as a whole is "absolutely erroneous and leads
to unjustifiable conclusions." Maternal mortality includes
all deaths related to pregnancy, including deaths from abortion; so the statistic suffers from the disadvantage of including the statistic with which it is compared. "Most women
who die from legal abortion are young," said Dr. Hilgers.
"The overwhelming majority of young women who die
from legal abortions are perfectly healthy, whereas a woman
who dies in childbirth dies from a disease or abnormality
which cannot be adequately treated."[19] Even if it were true
that legalization brought a reduction in the number of women who die as a result of abortion, it would make no
more sense than to legalize terrorist bombing on the ground
that terrorists sometimes injure or kill themselves with home-
made bombs.[20]

Most abortions today are performed surgically. The methods
are dilation and curettage and suction curettage for the
first twelve weeks of gestation, and saline injection and
hysterotomy in the later stages. In dilation and curettage
("D and C") the entrance to the womb is dilated and the
child is cut to pieces and removed. "In pregnancies beyond
the seventh week," wrote Dr. Alan Guttmacher, "fetal
parts are recognizable as they are removed piecemeal."[21]
The "fetal parts," of course, are arms, legs, and other
parts of what moments before was a living human being.
In suction abortion, a tube attached to a high-pressure
vacuum is inserted into the womb. The child is pulled
apart and the parts are sucked into a glass jar. The saline
method, originally developed in Nazi concentration camps,
involves withdrawal by needle of some of the amniotic fluid

in which the child rests and its replacement by a like quantity of a toxic saline solution which, because of its corrosive action, severely burns the skin of the child. Within 90 minutes his heart has usually stopped beating, and within 72 hours the mother goes into labor and delivers a dead baby. The hysterotomy abortion is a Caesarean section in which the abdomen is opened and the baby is lifted out. If the child is alive in the womb, he will be born alive by this method. A disposal problem is then presented. A few such babies have survived and have been placed for adoption; the others are smothered, drowned, or put aside to cry themselves to death.[22]

Permissive abortion is the logical outcome of positivism, secularism and the contraceptive mentality. The influence of contraceptive thinking can be seen in the status of the woman in an abortion climate. Contraception tends to reduce woman to the level of a sex object, having as her main function the gratification of others. But abortion is the ultimate exploitation of women by self-centered males. "The playboys of the western world," said Gloria Heffernan, M.D., "sacrifice their women in order to preserve their dream of libidinal freedom. It is the women who must go to surgery over and over again to insure this dream. The whimpering male refused to take responsibility for his sexual behavior. It is no surprise that Playboy Foundation money is now competing with Rockefeller Foundation money to promote the concept of permissive abortion. The rich man's solution has become the puerile male's solution and the last vestige of responsibility and commitment has disappeared."[23] Pope Paul VI warned about this in *Humanae Vitae*.

The emphasis on the "wanted child" implies that only "wanted" people have rights. To the extent that they are not wanted, they have no rights. Woman is not wanted as a partner but as a plaything and toys are usually not worth much. Moreover, it is now possible to determine the sex of unborn children. If the baby is the "wrong" sex, an abortion can be had. The irony is that most babies who are aborted for this reason are killed because they are girls. In one series of women who were tested and told the sex of their unborn children, 46 were told it was a girl and 29 chose to abort. Of 53 shown to be boys, only one was aborted.[24]

Women and babies are not the only victims of permissive abortion. One explanation for the spread of permissive abortion is that it is seen as a way to solve the welfare problem. In practical terms, it may be succeeding in this aim. A disproportionately large number of black babies is destroyed by abortion. In 1975, for example, about 300,000 blacks were aborted, or 1.3 percent of the black population.[25] This genocidal threat has aroused the opposition of Dick Gregory, Rev. Jesse Jackson, Cesar Chavez and other leaders of minority racial groups. The reality is that it is cheaper to kill a baby by abortion than to support him on welfare. The Godless state makes no effort to encourage self-control among welfare recipients; rather, its major concern is the prevention of troublesome and expensive offspring. Welfare minorities can achieve political dominance by reproducing themselves. Therefore, the only way the white masters, themselves unwilling to assume the responsibility of parenthood, can keep control is to induce or compel minorities to contracept, to sterilize, and, if necessary, to kill their own young.

The abortion of the future will be by pill, suppository, or some other do-it-yourself method. At that point the killing of a baby will be wholly elective and private. We have, finally, caught up with the pagan Romans who endowed the father, the paterfamilias, with the right to kill his child at his discretion. We give that right to the mother. But it is all the same to the victim.

10

Abortion: The Remedies

If you were outside the Golden Age Center that day in 1998 and you knew what was happening to the "useless" carpenter inside, what would you do? Would you break down the door and try to rescue him? Or would you go home and write a letter to your congressman? What *is* the remedy for legalized killing? Is it to rescue the victims? Or is it to lobby for a change in the law? Or both?

To put this in focus, we have to recall what the law has done with abortion. In *Roe* v. *Wade*[1] and *Doe* v. *Bolton*,[2] the Supreme Court ruled that the unborn child, throughout gestation, is not a "person" within the meaning of the Fourteenth Amendment which guarantees to persons the equal protection of the laws and the right not to be deprived by the state of life, liberty, or property without due process of law. The Court declined to decide whether the unborn child is a living human being. Instead, it ruled that, whether or not he is a human being, he is not a person. The ruling is therefore the same, in effect, as if the court had expressly held that a concededly human being is not a person. This was the first time the Supreme Court had

99

decided the issue of whether the unborn child is a person.

As the facts of life before birth became more widely understood in this century, state courts and lower federal courts recognized the personhood rights of the unborn child so as to enable him to inherit property (usually with the requirement that he be later born alive); to recover for personal injuries and even death suffered by him in the womb through the fault of another; and to call on the courts to protect his right to live, as where the courts would compel his mother to have a blood transufsion even over her religious objections.[3] The Supreme Court turned away from this developing line of cases and, in holding that the unborn child is a non-person, adopted the theory of the Dred Scott case,[4] where in 1857 the Supreme Court held that the free descendants of slaves could not be citizens and said that slaves were property rather than persons.

The framers of the Fourteenth Amendment clearly intended to reverse Dred Scott by ensuring that all human beings would be treated as persons.[5] But the Supreme Court, in the 1973 rulings, chose instead the rationale used for the Nazis' extermination of the Jews: that an innocent human being can be declared a non-person and deprived of life if his existence is inconvenient to others or if those others consider him unfit to live. In *Roe v. Wade,* the unborn child's right to live was asserted against the mother's privacy right to choose abortion. Between those two rights, the right to live would clearly prevail—which the court itself acknowledged in a footnote, indicating that if the personhood of the unborn child were established, abortion could not be allowed, even to save the life of the mother.[6] However, the court solved this problem by defining the unborn child as a non-person. Therefore he has no rights, and the only right that is left is his mother's right to privacy. The court claimed that this right is not absolute, but defined it so as to permit wholly permissive abortion at every stage of pregnancy to the time of normal delivery.

The Court divided pregnancy into trimesters and ruled that

1. During the "first trimester," the state may neither prohibit nor regulate abortion, except that it may require that the killing be done by a doctor. The Court has since decreed that, during the first trimester, the state may not require that the abortion be performed "in a hospital or a licensed health facility."[7]

2. During the stage after "the end of the first trimester" and until "viability," the state may not prohibit abortion but may regulate it "in ways that are reasonably related to maternal health."[8] The court defined viability as "the capability of meaningful life outside the mother's womb"[9] and said that "viability is usually placed at about seven months (28 weeks) but may occur earlier, even at 24 weeks."[10]

3. After viability the state may regulate abortion and may even prohibit it, except where it is necessary, "in appropriate medical judgment, for the preservation of the life or health of the mother."[11] The Court defined the health of the mother to include "psychological as well as physical well-being" and said that "the medical judgment may be exercised in the light of all factors—physical, emotional, psychological, familial, and the woman's age—relevant to the well-being of the mother.[12]

"Mental health" is a very loose criterion and the rulings are thus a license for elective abortion at every stage of pregnancy up to the time of normal delivery.

Under these rulings, the states have no authority to enact significant prohibitions of abortion. This was made clear in *Planned Parenthood* v. *Danforth,*[13] where the court struck down Missouri's requirements, applicable to first trimester abortions, that a married woman must have her husband's consent before killing their child by abortion and that an unmarried minor must have parental consent for having an abortion. The court upheld the Missouri requirement that a woman who has an abortion must give her consent in writing and that abortion facilities and doctors must keep records of the abortions performed, but it invalidated the Missouri requirement that the person performing an abortion must "exercise that degree of professional skill, care and diligence to preserve the life and health of the fetus which such person would be required to exercise in order to preserve the life and health of any fetus intended to be born and not aborted."[14] The Court noted that this statute would preclude abortion—perhaps indicating the Court's inclination to decide that the right to an abortion is the right to a dead baby and not merely the right to terminate a pregnancy. However, the Court indicated that this provision might be valid after viability.[15]

On June 21, 1977, the Supreme Court held that states that participate in the joint federal-state medical assistance program under Title XIX of the Social Security Act need not pay for abortions which are not "medically necessary" (psychiatric abortions are "medically necessary"), even when those states pay for childbirth;[16] and that a city regulation is valid which prohibits abortions in its municipal hospital except where there is "a threat of grave physiological injury or death to the mother."[17]

These 1977 decisions were criticized by the dissenting justices (Brennan, Marshall, Blackmun) as a retreat from *Roe* v. *Wade*—and perhaps they were, to some extent. More likely, the abortion-funding rulings were a reflection of the intrinsic difficulty involved if the Court were to order Congress to appropriate money for a specific purpose. Although the cases involved state appropriations, they are generally understood as meaning that it is up to Congress, rather than the court, to decide whether abortions will be funded from the public purse. It is more realistic to regard these funding cases as a reflection of the political delicacy of the Court's interfering in Congress' appropriating function, rather than as a retreat from the principles of *Roe* v. *Wade* or *Doe* v. *Bolton*. As *Planned Parenthood* v. *Danforth* indicates, *Wade* and *Bolton* are alive and well.

While there is always a possibility that the Supreme Court might reverse itself, it would be unrealistic to hold one's breath; we must therefore pursue other remedies. One possible remedy is a statutory definition of the unborn child as a "person," pursuant to Congress' power to enforce the Fourteenth Amendment. If Congress were to do this, it is likely that the statute would be held unconstitutional by the Supreme Court on the ground that the 1973 abortion rulings mean that the unborn child is incapable of being made a "person" under the Fourteenth Amendment. Nevertheless, the statutory definition of the unborn child as a person ought to be enacted. The Supreme Court is today essentially a political body and it might be disposed to yield to such a law if enough pressure were exerted by the public. Even if the Court were to rule the statute unconstitutional, the procedure could force the Court to clarify the theory of its pro-abortion rulings. To invalidate the statute, the Court would have to say, in effect, that the Fourteenth Amendment, which was designed to overrule the pro-slavery Dred Scott case, put a certain class of human beings, i.e., children in the womb, so far beyond the protection of the law that not even Congress could include them in it. If the Supreme Court were to follow the implications of *Roe* v. *Wade,* it would have to say just that. And there would be an advantage to forcing the Court thus to declare its position.

Another possible remedy for the abortion rulings is for Congress to withdraw the Supreme Court's jurisdiction to hear appeals in cases involving abortion. The Constitution in Article III, section 2, states that the Supreme Court has appellate jurisdiction, "with such Exceptions, and under such Regulations as the Congress shall make." Thus Congress definitely has the power to withdraw appellate jurisdiction from the Supreme Court in cases involving a particular subject.[18] This should be done with respect to abortion. Congress should also withdraw from lower federal courts the power to hear abortion cases. However, all this would be only a partial remedy. It would leave undisturbed the basic holdings of the Supreme Court's abortion cases. State courts would be likely to continue to follow those holdings as the latest authoritative interpretation of the United States Constitution. Withdrawal of Supreme Court and lower federal court jurisdiction over abortion would

leave the Supreme Court's abortion rulings intact as pre-
cedents. While a desirable move, such withdrawal of jurisdiction is therefore only a partial remedy.

Another desirable but partial remedy is the termination
of federal and state funding for abortions. The Supreme
Court decisions of 1977 indicate that neither Congress nor
the states will be compelled by the court to pay for abortions. Many rights are more readily available to the rich
than to the poor. The fact that the Supreme Court
has invented a constitutional right of a mother to kill her
baby does not mean that the taxpayers should be compelled to finance her decision. Today, the United States
government provides the major impetus for the abortion
movement through its direct funding of the Agency for
International Development and various domestic programs
and through its indirect subsidy of the anti-life activities
of the Rockefeller Foundation and other tax-privileged groups.
Public funding of abortion should be entirely terminated at
both the federal and the state level. However, this too is
but a partial remedy. The termination of government funding would not outlaw abortion. And it is not clear that the
Supreme Court would uphold a termination of funding which
did not leave room for funding "therapeutic" abortions,
including those sought for the mother's mental health.

The only certain constitutional remedy for the abortion
problem is a constitutional amendment. The Constitution
provides two methods of amendment. The first, the only
one that has ever been used, is for Congress to propose
the amendment by a two-thirds vote of each house and
then for the legislatures of three-fourths of the states to
ratify it. Or Congress could require that the ratification
be by conventions in the states rather than by the state
legislatures. Congress prescribed the convention method with
respect to the repeal of Prohibition but all other amendments have been ratified by the state legislatures.

The other method is for two-thirds (34) of the 50 state
legislatures to petition Congress to call a constitutional
convention. Congress would then be obliged to call the
convention, the members of which would be elected in

the states in the manner provided by Congress. The convention would then propose amendments which would become part of the Constitution when ratified by the legislatures of three-fourths (38) of the states (or by conventions in those states if Congress so directed). It seems clear that the 34 calls by the states must ask for a convention on the same general subject. It is likely that the convention would not be limited in the amendments it could propose to the states, but no recommendation would become part of the Constitution until it was ratified by 38 states.

With respect to the abortion amendment, it would be better for Congress to propose the amendment. However, a constitutional convention is a useful device with which to educate the public and force Congress to take action. State legislatures should call for a constitutional convention on the abortion issue. But the resolution must be a call for a convention. A resolution that would merely memorialize Congress to propose the amendment would be of no effect. The drive for a constitutional convention should be pursued simultaneously with the effort to have Congress propose the amendment itself. The objective is to get Congress to propose a strict amendment, not a watered-down compromise. And if Congress refuses to propose such an amendment, the convention should be held. The uncertainty involved in a constitutional convention is a small price to pay if that is the only way to remove the blight of legalized abortion from this land.

On the merits of the pro-life amendment itself, the basic principles are clear. The Declaration on Procured Abortion, issued with the approval of Pope Paul VI in 1974, states that human law "cannot declare to be right what would be opposed to the natural law, for this opposition suffices to give the assurance that a law is not a law at all." Therefor "a Christian can never conform to a law which is in itself immoral, and such is the case of a law which would admit in principle the liceity of abortion. Nor can a Christian take part in a propaganda campaign in favor of such a law, or vote for it."[19]

For a pro-life amendment to be worthy of support, three conditions have to be met:

1. The amendment, explicitly or by clear implication, must reverse the Supreme Court on its denial of personhood to the unborn, at least with reference to the right to live.

2. The amendment must restore constitutional protection to the right to live from the beginning of life, that is, from the moment of fertilization, and with those words, "moment of fertilization" (or words of equal precision). In *Roe V. Wade,* the Supreme Court indicated that it might regard "conception" as a "process over time, rather than an event."[20] The term "moment of conception," therefore is less satisfactory than "moment of fertilization," which unambiguously refers to the moment of joinder of sperm and ovum. If the amendment is ambiguous on this point, its protections might apply only at a later time than fertilization, such as implantation in the womb, which generally occurs about seven days after fertilization,[21] or viability, or whatever. Such ambiguity would legitimize early abortions by pill, suppository, or other means. If the constitutional protections do not attach at fertilization, there will be no constitutional obstacle to licensing such pills and devices for use at an early stage of pregnancy. And if those abortifacients are licensed for use at any early stage, they will be available for use at every stage.

3. The amendment should permit no exceptions to its prohibition of abortion. An exception clause is not needed to permit removal of an ectopic pregnancy or a cancerous womb in an appropriate case where the mother's life is imminently threatened, since they have never been considered abortions in the eyes of the law. Beyond these cases, which need no specific exception, it would be wrong to write into our Constitution the principle that one may kill an innocent nonaggressor to save his or her own life. That principle, based on the notion that might makes right, is contrary to sound

morality as well as the precedent of the common law. On the practical level, moreover, it is impossible to draft an exception clause in a constitutional amendment on abortion that would not be broad enough to authorize psychiatric abortions, for example, where the doctor says there is a chance the mother will kill herself or suffer great mental harm if she does not kill her unborn baby.

With these criteria in mind, let us examine the major amendments that have been proposed. There are two basic types, the states' rights amendment and the prohibitory amendment.

The states' rights approach was introduced by Representative Leonor K. Sullivan (D., Mo.) in 1975: "The Congress within Federal jurisdiction and the several states within their jurisdictions shall have power to protect life including the unborn at every stage of biological development irrespective of age, health, or condition of physical dependency."[22] The first problem with the states' rights amendment is that it would not overrule the basic holding of the Supreme Court that the unborn child is a non-person. It would permit, but not require Congress and the states "to protect life including the unborn." They could then decide whether to forbid or allow abortion within their respective jurisdictions. For a time, the states' rights amendment could cause some reduction in the total number of legal abortions. But in the long run it would probably increase rather than decrease the toll in unborn human lives. Abortion mills would be created in some states and their number and volume of business would expand despite the efforts of other states to forbid abortion within their own borders.

More importantly, the states' rights amendment would write into the Constitution the totalitarian idea that innocent human beings hold their lives at the discretion of legislative majorities. For this reason, the amendment is morally and intellectually bankrupt. It would be like fighting World War II for the principle that each locality in Germany should have the right to decide whether to have its own death camp. Innocent life would become a subject of political negotiation and bartering, just like a highway or school appropriation. The amendment, moreover, would endanger, in addition to the unborn, the lives of the senile, the retarded and other vulnerable classes through its implication that there is a "power," but not a duty, "to protect life at whatever stage." The momentum of the anti-life principle it would write into the Constitution would soon increase the casualties, not only among the unborn but among others as well.

Apart from its intrinsic failings, the states' rights amendment is a political dead end. Some well-meaning but befuddled opponents of abortion advocate it as a necessary concession to political reality. They say it is the best we can get and that it is better to save some lives than to permit the slaughter to continue unabated while we haggle over details of a visionary constitutional amendment that will never get on the books. The fact, however, is that if the states' rights amendment were ever submitted to the states, it would have to be opposed by the strongest elements in the pro-life movement. For the state's rights amendment, in its self-contradiction, is essentially anti-life. It could never be adopted against the opposition of those who believe that innocent life is not negotiable.

The second, or prohibitory, type of constitutional amendment, is the only one that is politically feasible and that can be supported in principle. Such an amendment, generally called a "human life amendment," was proposed by the National Right to Life Committee and introduced in Congress in 1977 by Senator Jake Garn (R. Utah):

Section 1. With respect to the right to life, the word "person", as used in this article and in the fifth and fourteenth articles of amendment to the Constitution of the United States, applies to all human beings, irrespective of age, health, function, or condition of dependency, including their unborn offspring at every stage of their biological development.

Section 2. No unborn person shall be deprived of life by any person: Provided, however, that nothing in this article shall prohibit a law permitting only those medical procedures required to prevent the death of the mother.

Section 3. Congress and the several States shall have the power to enforce this article by appropriate legislation within their respective jurisdictions.[23]

This amendment would restore personhood to the unborn, but it is defective in two major respects. First, it is ambiguous as to the time the protections attach. The unborn child would have to be an "offspring," a term that is generally applied to a later stage in gestation.[24] This amendment may therefore provide protection only at implantation or even later.[25] It does not clearly protect life from the very beginning, which is the moment of fertilization.

The second defect in this amendment is its wide open exception clause which would permit abortion in any case where a doctor declared it was "required to prevent the death of the mother." It would in effect authorize psychiatric abortions since in a prosecution it would be practically impossible to overcome that professional judgment of the certifying physician, even though pregnant women have a lower suicide rate than nonpregnant women.[26]

Finally, as an incidental point, under the first clause of Section 2 ("No unborn person shall be deprived of life by any person"), it could be a violation of the Constitution for a driver to be innocently involved in an automobile accident in which a woman suffers a miscarriage.

The defects of the National Right to Life Committee amendment are remediable. Section 2 should be removed and Section 1 should be re-worded so as to apply at the moment of fertilization. But unless it is corrected, the amendment is unworthy of support. In fact, as it now reads, it must be opposed.

The other major type of prohibitory amendment is typified by the amendment introduced in 1977 by Senator Jesse

Helms (R., N.C.):

> Section 1. With respect to the right to life guaranteed in this Constitution, every human being, subject to the jurisdiction of the United States, or of any State, shall be deemed, from the moment of fertilization, to be a person and entitled to the right to life.
>
> Section 2. Congress and the several States shall have concurrent power to enforce this article by appropriate legislation.[27]

The Helms Amendment is sound. It attaches the protections "from the moment of fertilization." It says nothing about exceptions because nothing need be said about them in a constitutional amendment. Rather, it would restore personhood where the Supreme Court denied it, with respect to the right to life. The life of the unborn person would be protected by the impartial application of the constitutional principles applicable to all persons. He could not be legally killed for any reason that would not permit the killing of his elder brother, his grandmother or any other innocent person.

The Helms Amendment would authorize the states to prohibit abortion. But it would go further by requiring them to do so. If a state were to exclude a specific class of persons from the protection of the criminal law, it would deny equal protection of the law to that class. For example, a law that would punish the homicide of all persons except Jews or those over the age of 70 would be unconstitutional. So would a law that failed to prohibit the homicide of unborn persons. Under the Helms Amendment the unborn child would no longer be a non-person whose life is of no constitutional account; he would again be guaranteed the equal treatment that is his due. At the same time, the amendment would not require that unborn children be counted in the census, that they have passports, etc.; these administrative matters are properly subject to legislative discretion with or without an amendment. The amendment would restore personhood with respect to the right to life, which was the only issue on which the Supreme Court squarely denied it.

It should be remembered, however, that the Helms Amendment is not sacrosanct; other language could be formulated to do the same job.[28] No amendment will be perfect but three elements are essential:

1. The amendment must restore personhood to the unborn child with respect to the right to live.
2. It must clearly apply from the beginning of life, which is the moment of fertilization; and
3. Its prohibition of abortion must contain no exception.

Besides promotion of a strict human life amendment, several other things should be done. A priority task is to support Birthright and similar groups which provide help to girls and women with problem pregnancies. The pro-life movement is not an academic exercise; its business is saving lives. Mere opposition to abortion is insufficient without financial and professional help for people in trouble. It is also important to lessen the stigma attached to girls who choose to keep their children who were conceived out of wedlock. This is not to condone immorality. Rather, a girl who chooses—against the usual pressures of family and friends—to let her baby live deserves respect and help. Counseling is important, but it cannot take the place of material help when that is needed. "And if a brother or a sister be naked and in want of daily food, and one of you say to them, 'Go in peace, be warmed and filled,' yet you do not give them what is necessary for the body, what does it profit?" [Jas 2:15-17]. As Bishop William E. McManus of Fort Wayne-South Bend, Indiana, said: "Our diocese has budgeted funds to pay whatever expenses a financially troubled pregnant woman requires to give birth to her baby. If these diocesan funds run out, more will be raised. No woman who comes to us will even be tempted to say she is too poor to have her baby."[29]

Another important task is to speak plainly: abortion is murder, and it does no good to soften that fact. For historical reasons, the crime of abortion was not defined as murder in criminal statutes or at common law. However, abortion is murder in the moral sense because it is the directly intended taking of human life without justification. Pope Pius XI referred to abortion as "the direct murder of the innocent."[30] Those who commit abortion commit murder in this moral sense, regardless of criminal statutes and the Supreme Court's decisions. Thus Rev. Christian Bartholdy, the Danish Lutheran leader, said in 1965 that widespread abortion was turning his country into "a nation of murderers."[31] Some dissident theologians object to describing abortion as murder because the Church has never defined the exact moment at which the soul is infused, and they make much of the fact that science does not yet understand how identical twins develop, before or after implantation, from what had appeared to be only one fertilized ovum. But just because science can not be certain how many human beings are present before implantation, it is nevertheless true that from the very moment of fertilization there is at least *one* human being. Although the Church has not precisely defined the moment at which the soul is infused, theological speculation on this point can have no effect on the morality of abortion from the very moment of fertilization.

The Declaration on Procured Abortion states that "right from fertilization is begun the adventure of human life. . . . From a moral point of view this is certain: even if a doubt existed concerning whether the fruit of conception is already a human person, it is objectively a grave sin to dare to risk murder. 'The one who will be a man is already one.'"[32] The Second Vatican Council affirmed that "from the moment of its conception life must be guarded with the greatest care, while abortion and infanticide are unspeakable crimes."[33] Without passing judgment on anyone's subjective culpability, one must assert that in the objective moral sense, the abortionist and those who procure his crime are murderers. "The simple fact," said Dietrich Bonhoeffer, "is that God certainly intended to create a human being and that this nascent human being has been deliberately deprived of his life. And that is nothing but murder."[34] Abortionists deserve the same respect to which any other murderer is entitled, as do judges who acquiesce in the killings. They deserve no more respect than the judges in Germany who closed their eyes to the murder of Jews, Gypsies, Poles and other minorities. In his dissent in the 1977 abortion-funding cases, Justice Blackmun (joined by Justices Brennan and Marshall) complained about "the demonstrated wrath and noise of the abortion opponents."[35] The Justices have earned that wrath. The Nuremberg trial records indicate that many doctors participated in the Nazis' exterminations because they feared the loss of esteem of their colleagues.[36] Because similar factors appear to be at work in this country, it behooves us to show the abortionists and their protectors, on the bench and elsewhere in politics, that the scorn of those who value the right to live is more to be feared than the esteem of their confederates in murder is to be sought.

Abortion presents a difficult issue of civil disobedience. In October, 1977, a local Virginia court found several opponents of abortion not guilty of the charge that they had committed criminal trespass by a sit-in that obstructed the operation of an abortion clinic. The judge accepted their plea that they were acting in the honest belief that their trespass was necessary to save innocent lives.[37] However, this ruling probably will not be followed. Although the common-law privilege of necessity would justify one in entering somebody's house to prevent the latter from knifing a person to death, it would not justify intrusion to prevent him from destroying his own property. And it is likely that most courts would not allow trespassers to claim that their belief that human life was at stake is reasonable in the face of the clear and well-known holding of the Supreme Court that unborn children are not persons and therefore are not entitled to the right to live. Legally—according to the Supreme Court—the life of the unborn child is practically as much at the disposal of his mother as would be the life of a gold-fish. There is therefore no legal right for any third party to interfere to prevent an abortion.

In moral terms, however, there seems to be a right to interfere in a situation where there is a reasonable prospect that such interference would be more than a Quixotic gesture and would actually save lives. But we have to be careful not to exaggerate this point. The primary remedy still lies in the amendment of the Constitution to prohibit abortion, and this legal route still offers the best chance to reverse the Supreme Court rulings. However, the tactics of demon-stration and even obstruction cannot be wholly ruled out. The experience of the civil rights and anti-war movements confirms the efficacy of such tactics. And abortion involves a more direct and locally identifiable injustice.

The laws which protect abortion clinics against those who would prevent abortions provide a legal sanctuary for murder. Those laws, therefore, are unjust and morally void, as are the Supreme Court's abortion rulings. Whether demonstra-tion and obstruction should be used against abortion facili-ties is therefore a question of prudence and tactics. While the main thrust of the pro-life movement is legal, it is time to give serious consideration to more direct action. However, prudence dictates that any activity of this sort be carried out in a manner that is likely to be effective, rather than to damage the cause by leading it to frustration and disre-pute. The most desirable technique would be a continued pray-er vigil outside the abortion premises, with the distribution of pro-life literature to those entering the premises and to passersby. There could be situations where it would be appropriate to enter the premises but this would generally be counterproductive. In any event, personal injury and property damage must be avoided, and isolated "kamikaze" actions would do more harm than good.

The overall objective is not to confront abortion with the mere strength of numbers or with physical force. It is instead to dramatize the opposition of abortion to the law of God and to pray publicly at the scene of the crime that God will remove this blight from our land. With the power of the state arrayed on the side of death, there is practically nothing one can do to save the life of the child whose mother is resolved upon his death. Breaking up the furniture will be of virtually no use in this respect. Our reliance here must be on the Rosary rather than the sledgehammer.

A nationally coordinated program would be most appropriate and the Catholic bishops are the ones who should properly initiate it and lead it through prudent and peaceful demonstrations. If such demonstrations prove to be counter to the civil law, the Bishops and their followers ought to be willing to pay the penalty.

The civil rights leaders in the 1960s accomplished much because they were willing to go to jail in protest against laws they regarded as unjust. When the right to life is at stake, the Catholic Bishops ought at least to be willing to do the same. And members of their flock should be willing to go with them. We could make good use of a book of "Letters from the County Jail," written by the Ordinary of the Diocese.

11

Euthanasia

It was March 28, 1976—Mother's Day in Britain. "It isn't cowardly, Mum, for goodness' sake," said 60-year-old Yolande McShane to her 87-year-old mother in her bedroom in the nursing home. "If you had a dog in this state you would take it to the vet, wouldn't you?"

"A dog hasn't got a soul," replied the mother. "I'm so afraid of being punished after."

"Oh, Mummy, for this? You wouldn't be punished for this . . . don't be having any doubts. . . . Don't bungle it, Mummy, don't make a mess of it." The daughter then handed her mother a lethal dose of fifteen barbiturate tablets, urged her to take them with a "big drink of whiskey, that's always fatal, Mum," and walked out of the room.

As soon as the daughter left, the nursing-home nuns rushed in and snatched the pills from the mother, who was about to take them. The whole episode had been filmed by a hidden police camera and Yolande McShane was sentenced to two years for aiding and abetting an attempted suicide. The British court accepted the police film as evidence. Later, British television built a documentary around

117

the episode and showed it to home viewers. The daughter's
motive was allegedly the $70,000 she was to inherit on her
mother's death. While the daughter was serving her sen-
tence, the mother died of natural causes and the daughter
got the legacy.[1]

The McShane case is an extreme example. Nevertheless,
it may be instructive for our future. The mother was a
burden on the daughter, who also sought financial gain
from her death. Similarly, with our aging population, there
is a limit to the willingness of the young and middle-aged
to pay taxes for the maintenance of aged nonproducers.
In 1977, one beneficiary was drawing Social Security for
every three workers who were paying into the system. By
2030 the ratio will be one for two.[2] A complicating factor
is that medical costs will keep rising as the population
ages, because the elderly require more medical care. These
financial pressures probably account for much of the current
interest in euthanasia in this country.

"Euthanasia" is derived from the Greek and means "hap-
py death." Euthanasia can be voluntary, with the consent
of the victim, or involuntary. It can be active, where the
victim is shot, poisoned, or otherwise killed by active intervention, or passive, where treatment is refused by the
victim or withheld from him.

Active euthanasia, which is murder committed by active
means, such as the administration of poison, is never permissible in law or morality. Nor is passive euthanasia
through the withholding of *ordinary* means of life support,
such as food or routine medication. However, with respect
to truly *extraordinary* means of life support, the Church
teaches that they may be used, but there is no oblication
to do so; their use is optional. In his address on November
24, 1957, Pope Pius XII stated it this way:

> The rights and duties of the family depend in general
> upon the presumed will of the unconscious patient if he is
> of age and *sui juris*. Where the proper and independent
> duty of the family is concerned, they are usually bound

only to the use of ordinary means.

Consequently, if it appears that the attempt at resuscitation constitutes in reality such a burden for the family that one cannot in all conscience impose it upon them, they can lawfully insist that the doctor should discontinue these attempts, and the doctor can lawfully comply. There is not involved here a case of direct disposal of the life of the patient, nor of euthanasia in any way: this would never be licit. Even when it causes the arrest of circulation, the interruption of attempts at resuscitation is never more than an indirect cause of the cessation of life, and one must apply in this case the principle of double effect and of "voluntarium in causa."

Death is not the greatest evil, and there is a time when it is proper to acquiesce in its victory. We have a duty to preserve life, but death is the door to eternal life and it can be wrong for doctors and even a family to turn the process of dying into a technological circus. To say this is not to depreciate the sanctity of life. Rather, it is to recognize that death must come and that, at some point, extreme measures of resistance are neither necessary nor appropriate.

A person dies in stages, and we can tentatively describe the process as follows. First is clinical death, the cessation of spontaneous respiration and circulation. The heart and lungs no longer function on their own. The common law generally accepted this as the legal definition of death.[3] When respiration and circulation cease, the brain is deprived of oxygen and circulating blood and it soon dies, unless respiration and circulation are induced by resuscitative procedures. The brain itself dies in stages:

First the cortex ceases to function and then the midbrain and brainstem die. If there is irreversible destruction of the higher levels of the nervous system, there is permanent loss of consciousness, but cardiorespiratory function can go on, sometimes unaided but sometimes only with artificial aids, so that the life of the body now depends solely on a machine. When besides cortical death, the midbrain and the brainstem are irreversibly damaged, it still may be possible to maintain cardiovascular function for some time through stimulation of the vasomotor reflexes. Ultimately, when all the components of the brain are dead, biological death, or permanent extinction of bodily life occurs. Thereafter, the process of cellular death begins, and, because of differences in cellular composition, the death of different parts of the body occurs at different times.[4]

There are vegetative and sapient brain functions. The vegetative activity of the brain controls such things as breathing, chewing, swallowing, sleeping, and waking. We also have

> a more highly developed brain which is uniquely human which controls our relation to the outside world, our capacity to talk, to see, to feel, to sing, to think. Brain death necessarily must mean the death of both of these functions of the brain, vegetative and the sapient. Therefore, the presence of any function which is regulated or governed or controlled by the deeper parts of the brain which in laymen's terms might be considered purely vegetative would mean that the brain is not biologically dead.[5]

Death is the extinction of life. It is the breaking up of an entity into its component parts. The death of a human being is the separation of the soul from the body. When this occurs, the body dies in that it decomposes or breaks up into its component parts. The sequence of death, therefore, is clinical death, brain death, and cellular death or the death of the component parts of the body. When a particular human being dies is a medical question. In his November, 1957 address, Pope Pius XII said:

> Where the verification of the fact in particular cases is concerned, the answer cannot be deduced from any religious and moral principle and, under this aspect, does not fall within the competence of the Church. Until an answer can be given, the question must remain open. But

considerations of a general nature allow us to believe that human life continues for as long as its vital functions—distinguished from the simple life of organs—manifest themselves spontaneously or even with the help of artificial processes.

In 1968 a special faculty committee at Harvard University recommended that "brain death" be accepted as the criterion for death. The committee recommended that brain death be certified by the following tests and observations:

1. Total lack of response to even the most painful external stimuli.
2. No spontaneous muscular movements or breathing for one hour.
3. No bodily reflexes, and the pupils of the eyes are fixed and dilated.
4. A flat brain-wave pattern on the electroencephalogram, indicating the absence of brain activity.

The tests and observations should be repeated at least 24 hours later. But the criteria do not apply if the body has been chilled below 90°F. or if the central nervous system had been affected by depressants such as barbiturates.[6] These criteria are not infallible, however, and further refinements have been suggested.

The definition of death is especially important with respect to organ transplants. The traditional definition of death as irreversible cessation of all vital functions, including respiration and circulation, can make it difficult to transplant an organ successfully. If the doctor must wait until respiration and heartbeat have ceased, the organ will probably have begun to deteriorate. The Uniform Anatomical Gift Act (adopted as such or by similar legislation in all fifty states) does not define the point at which death occurs, but leaves that question to whatever solution is consistent with generally accepted medical standards.[7]

It is possible for the brain to cease functioning irreversibly while respiration and circulation are maintained by artificial mechanisms. If this occurs, may the still-beating heart be removed? It may, if brain death is conclusive and the patient is therefore dead.

Whether or not a transplant is involved, if brain death is accepted as a test of death, its occurrence will permit the mechanisms to be turned off. An example is the case of Mrs. Celia Cain in Jacksonville, Florida, who had suffered brain death and was on a respirator. A judge, at the request of her family, ordered the respirator turned off, and her heart and lungs stopped minutes later. The judge acted after a doctor testified that "breath is being sustained and blood is being pumped through the veins and heart of a dead person."[8]

Many states have enacted statutes that recognize brain death as a test for death.[9] One purpose of these laws is to protect attending physicians from malpractice suits, particularly in organ transplants where an organ is removed after brain death but while respiration and circulation (the old criteria for death) are maintained artificially. The statutes vary. Some provide that brain death is merely one criterion. Others establish it as a mandatory test: if brain death occurs, death must be pronounced. There is nothing wrong in principle with a statute that defines death; however, there is a practical objection in that science will probably develop new criteria and such statutes will become outmoded and sources of confusion. They attempt to confine the exercise of sound medical judgment within a static formula. If the criteria for death are to be defined by statute, they should include a general provision such as the following (which is contained in the Ethical and Religious Directives for Catholic Health Facilities, issued by the Catholic bishops of the United States in 1971): "The determination of the time of death must be made in accordance with responsible and commonly accepted scientific criteria."

Another serious objection to the brain-death statutes is the "wedge" argument, that such legislation is the opening move in a campaign to remove the protection of the law from the terminally ill, the retarded, and similar classes.

Further, a statutory definition of brain death could tend to confuse the issue of early abortions. Brain activity is detectable in the child in the womb at about six weeks, yet he is alive from the moment of fertilization. Brain activity may be the last sign of life but it surely is not the first and thus it should not be regarded as the sole determinant of life. No statute should overemphasize the flat reading on the electroencephalogram so as to obscure the fact that brain death also requires the loss of reflexes, spontaneous movement, breathing and response to stimuli.

A potential issue of human dignity also arises. Human bodies with dead brains can be kept artifically breathing and respirating for the purpose of testing them and "harvesting" their spare parts, as Dr Willard Gaylin of Columbia University has proposed.[10] Such use of a truly dead body is not inherently wrong, but it can tend toward a mechanical view of human nature and diminished reverence for life. This tendency could be increased by a statutory sanction of brain death.

Statutory definition of brain death is unnecessary and potentially confusing. It would be preferable—all things considered—for the definition of death to be considered a matter for medical science, rather than the legislature, to determine. The courts, of course, should be vigilant to intervene to safeguard life against abuses of medical judgment in this area.

The other statutory intrusion into the process of dying is the "living will" or "death with dignity" legislation. These laws, enacted in several states, generally provide that a competent person may execute a written document requesting that life-support mechanisms and treatments not be administered to him in the event that he becomes hopelessly ill. There are numerous variations among the existing and proposed laws.[11] Some require that the request be executed in advance of the illness in question; others that it be at or about the same time as the proposed withdrawal or withholding of treatment. They vary also on the right of family members to decline treatment for an incompetent or comatose patient, and some might be interpreted to permit the withholding of ordinary as well as extraordinary means of support.

To the extent that such laws provide only for withholding or withdrawing extraordinary means of treatment, they are unnecessary because the uncodified common law already permits this. Indeed, such a statute may lead to the reverse impression, that even extraordinary means should not be withdrawn unless specific authorization has been given pursuant to the statute. If these laws provide for withholding or withdrawing ordinary means of support, they are unnecessary as far as the competent adult is concerned, since he already has the right (in principle) to decline ordinary means of support even when they are necessary to save his life. However, to the extent that new laws permit the next of kin to decline the use of ordinary treatment on behalf of incompetent or minor patients, they open the door to abuse. They could legalize the elimination of the incurable and the useless. The next step would be to authorize active euthanasia, which would be nothing but legalized homicide.

Such laws are unsound in that they intrude the state into an area of medical judgment where the limited function of the state should be to intervene only in cases of abuse to protect life. They are an opening wedge, designed "to get legislation on the books dealing with the easier cases first."[12] These unnecessary laws erode the concept that medical treatment should clearly depend on informed consent. If treatment is withheld or withdrawn on the strength of a previously executed document, that previ-.ous intent may not correspond to the intent of the patient at the time of crisis, particularly if he is unable to communicate. And if the intent of the patient is declared at the time of the crisis, it ought to be regarded as unreliable. When one is under the stress of dying and his judgment is influenced by pain or pain-killing drugs, he ought not to be routinely presumed competent to buy a house, let alone to consign himself to eternity.

"Death with dignity" laws have a built-in bias in favor

of letting a patient die if he has executed the required
document rather than taking even ordinary means to save
him. Moreover, doctors who have learned the art of killing
by abortion will not scruple to dispose of the elderly,
especially when they are paid to do so by the family and,
as a practical matter, are protected by the law.

The Karen Quinlan case brought the entire euthanasia
question to the fore. On April 15, 1975, Karen, then 21
years old, was admitted to Newton Memorial Hospital in
New Jersey in a coma from unknown causes. She was im-
mediately placed on a respirator and, nine days later, was
transferred to St. Clare's Hospital in Denville for tests.
At no time did she suffer brain death, although extensive
brain damage was apparent, resulting in permanent loss of
sapient brain activity. Her parents, Joseph and Julia Quinlan,
asked the attending physicians to discontinue the life-support
mechanisms. They refused, and since Karen was an adult
receiving care at public expense, the parents could not
order them to do so and could not change doctors. So the
parents went to court. The doctors agreed that Karen was
comatose and in "a chronic and persistent vegetative state,
having no awareness of anything or anyone around her
and existing at a primitive reflex level." The sapient activity
of her brain apparently was irreversibly lost, but she continued to have vegetative brain activity and was therefore
not dead.

The Quinlans, who had adopted Karen when she was a
child, sought to have Joseph Quinlan, the adoptive father,
declared guardian of the girl for the purpose of terminating
the treatment. They acted on the opinion of their pastor
and bishop that the life-sustaining treatment was extraordinary and therefore optional and not required. The hospital and attending physicians opposed the Quinlans' petition.

The trial court held against the parents. The New Jersey
Supreme Court, reversing the trial court, decided for the
Quinlans.[13] The Supreme Court seemed to adopt the distinction between ordinary and extraordinary treatment. The distinction between them, in the court's view, appeared to be

the possibility of cure. Therefore, "one would have to think that the use of the same respirator or like support could be considered 'ordinary' in the context of the possibly curable patient but 'extra-ordinary' in the context of the forced sustaining by cardiorespiratory process of an irreversibly doomed patient." The court recommended that ethics committees be formed in hospitals to aid in making these decisions. (The Supreme Judicial Court of Massachusetts, in another case, rejected the "ethics committee' approach and said the courts should make the decisions.)[14]

Joseph Quinlan was appointed guardian of Karen, with full power to change doctors and:

> Upon the concurrence of the guardian and family of Karen, should the responsible attending physicians conclude that there is no reasonable possibility of Karen's ever emerging from the present comatose condition to a cognitive, sapient state and that the life-support apparatus now being administered to Karen should be discontinued, they shall consult with the hospital "Ethics Committee" or like body of the institution in which Karen is then hospitalized. If that consultative body agrees that there is no reasonable possibility of Karen's ever emerging from her present comatose condition to a cognitive, sapient state, the present lifesupport system may be withdrawn and said action shall be without any civil or criminal liability therefor on the part of any participant, whether guardian, physician, hospital, or others.

On the facts of the case, the holding in *Matter of Quinlan* is justifiable. The Quinlans formed their consciences carefully and reached a conclusion consistent with Catholic teaching. Given the extraordinary character of the treatment (a highly debatable point), they were morally at liberty to continue or discontinue it. The court's ruling is technically justifiable. However, for several reasons it was a bad ruling.

The opinion of the court is so open-ended that it blurs the distinction between ordinary and extraordinary treatment and opens the door to withdrawal of ordinary means of support from those who are in a vegetative state. The court's criterion for discontinuance of treatment was the presence or absence of a reasonable possibility of "Karen's ever emerging from her present comatose condition to a cognitive, sapient state"—but if cognition and sapience are the criteria for the right to go on living, the severely retarded and the senile aged are in jeopardy. The New York *Times* editorialized that the Quinlan ruling "suggests sanction for terminating extraordinary and hopeless efforts to prolong the life of cancer patients wracked with pain or of victims of neurological disease who have lost control of their motor functions. Just how far such 'mercy killing' can be condoned remains for future judges to decide." [15] The court further opened this door when it indicated that a court order is not necessary for doctors to apply the Quinlan decision to future cases: "By the above ruling we do not intend to be understood as implying that a proceeding for judicial declaratory relief is necessarily required for the implementation of comparable decisions in the field of medical practice."

The Quinlan case should not have been brought to court. Even when the suit was brought, the court should have declined to interfere. The imprudence of the litigation was dramatized by the fact that, after Mr. Quinlan changed doctors and the life-support mechanisms were withdrawn, Karen did not die. At this writing, two full years after the court's decision, she is still alive, surviving without the life-support mechanisms which were withdrawn.

In any event, the precedential value of the Quinlan ruling is lessened because it was based on the premise that "removal from the respirator would cause her death soon." [16] In their brief to the New Jersey Supreme Court, the Quinlans' attorneys stated as facts that "without the respirator Karen would die . . . and even with the aid of the respirator she will not live for so long as another year." If the only function of a respirator is to hold off the imminent death of someone who will probably never come out of a coma and would quickly die without it, the respirator should more readily be regarded as extraordinary than if is is providing life support to one who, though likely never to recover, is not in immediate danger of death without it. Doctors, the family, lawyers, and even judges can be wrong. The question of Karen's capacity to survive without the respirator was one of the crucial facts of the case. And in its rush to intervene on the side of death, the court was in error on this fact.

The Quinlan ruling is the leading case that permits a guardian to refuse or terminate medical treatment on behalf of his unconscious or incompetent ward.[17] It is also evidence of the modern tendency to look to statutes and the courts for the solution to moral problems.

The courts are equipped to deal with euthanasia only when there is active killing by poisoning or other means or when clearly ordinary means of life support are withdrawn or withheld. A situation of the latter type would be the withholding of food or routine antibotics from a retarded child. In 1971, doctors at John Hopkins Hospital permitted a newborn Mongoloid to starve to death, with the concurrence of his parents, when the latter refused their consent to a minor operation to remove an intestinal blockage.[18] In a 30-month period, 43 defective infants were allowed to die at Yale New Haven Hospital.[19] In such cases the courts should intervene on the side of life, not death.

A competent adult has the legal right, at least in theory, to refuse even ordinary means of medical treatment and life support,[20] but minors and incompetent adults need special protection. Where the family and the doctors disagree on the withdrawal of life-support measures, the courts should not intervene, even if one side is acting unreasonably. This refusal to intervene would be a pro-life decision, since the measures would be removed only if the family and the doctors concur. In cases of clear abuse, an agreement by the family and the doctor to remove the support should be subject to judicial intervention, particularly where the family has "shopped around" for a compliant doctor.

To argue that the law should not intrude into medical judgment is not to say that all doctors should be unreservedly trusted. The Nazi exterminations were the invention of psychiatrists and other doctors, more than of Hitler and his bureaucrats.[21] Moreover, doctors, the secular "priests" of our day, are probably more expedient and liable to despair than any other group. Physicians "are twice as prone to suicide as either professional-technical persons or the general population," and half of the suicidal deaths among physicians "occur during the most productive phases of a physician's life, namely 35–54 years of age."[22] The law should act on behalf of life in restraining doctors who would abuse their position. In management of the dying, control of reproduction, and manipulation of genes, the medical profession bears watching, as do the lawyers in the legislatures and the courts. Unfortunately, the movement toward legislation in the matter of dying reflects a tendency of those two groups to liberate each other from the restraints of the moral law and common sense.

The increased and favorable interest in euthanasia is a reflection of philosophical and spiritual bankruptcy. As positivists, we are no longer certain that it is always wrong to kill an innocent, helpless person. As secularists, we have lost sight of the God who rewards and punishes. Our contraceptive mentality has conditioned us to regard inconvenient life as not good, and our experience with abortion has hardened us to killing. A recent survey by sociologist William McCready of the National Opinion Research Center indicates that acceptance of voluntary euthanasia is increasing among Catholics who "agree that artificial contraception is permissible" and who "favor the legalizing of abortion."[23] This should not be surprising. When we no longer regard life as sacred and good, we have already started down the slippery slope toward euthanasia.

The age of the Merciful Release will come in stages, not all at once. First we will be presented with the 85-year-old man, incurably ill and racked with pain, beyond the power of drugs to cure or to alleviate his pain. He has no family, or—worse yet—his family is being driven to poverty by medical bills. He writhes on his bed of pain and begs, "Doctor, please let me go." Are we going to insist that he suffer? If we will not allow the doctor to give him release by active means or the termination of even ordinary treatment, are we not heartless and cruel? So we make a small exception.

But what about the old man in the next bed? He is just as terminal, just as pain-racked, just as far beyond the power of drugs to cure or to alleviate his pain. His family situation is fully as serious. In every respect, he is as badly off as the first man—but in one respect he is worse. He cannot communicate. Are we going to give a Merciful Release to the first man but deny it to the second, because he cannot ask for it? So we make a second exception.

But what about the old man in the third bed? He is not in pain. He is not even sick. He is sitting in bed, eating cheese and crackers and watching Monday night football. He does not want to die. But if he knew what was good for him he would.

This may sound far-fetched, but the pioneer "death with dignity" bill, introduced by Representative Walter W. Sackett Jr., a medical doctor in the Florida legislature in 1971, provided that any person might execute a document asking for "death with dignity," which was broadly defined to include active euthanasia as well as withdrawal of even ordinary means of life support. In the event the person is "unable to make such a decision because of mental or physical incapacity," a spouse or a majority of his first-degree kin could request it for him. In the case of a wealthy person, this could make for interesting maneuvers by the beneficiaries of his estate. Legal "incapacity," a technical condition, can exist even if the subject holds a job and goes about his daily business. Under Sackett's bill, the beneficiary of "death with dignity" would not even have to be sick. If "any person is disabled and there is no kinship" available, "death with dignity shall be granted any person if in the opinion of three (3) physicians the prolongation of life is meaningless."[24]

Later, Dr. Sackett toned down his bill considerably. But its original version is a window on our future. Those who regard some lives as not worth living are incipient directors of the Golden Age Center in 1998.

In 1920, Karl Binding and Alfred Hoch, a German law professor and psychiatrist, wrote *The Release of the Destruction of Life Devoid of Value.* The book argued that there is such a thing as a "life not worth living" and it influenced the pre-Hitler generation. In 1934, after Hitler came to power, a German court legalized abortion for defectives. When euthanasia was proposed—for the good of the victims—it was hardly foreseen what the end would be.

Justice Robert H. Jackson of the United States Supreme Court, chief of counsel for the prosecution in the Nuremberg trials of Nazi war criminals, wrote as follows in his foreword for the record of the Hadamar trial:

A freedom-loving people will find in the records of the war crimes trials instruction as to the roads which lead to such a regime and the subtle first steps that must be avoided. Even the Nazis probably would have surprised themselves, and certainly they would have shocked many German people, had they proposed as a single step to establish the kind of extermination institution that the evidence shows the Hadamar Hospital became. But the end was not thus reached; it was achieved in easy stages.

To begin with, it involved only the incurably sick, insane and mentally deficient patients of the institution. It was easy to see that they were a substantial burden to society, and life was probably of little comfort to them. It is not difficult to see how, religious scruples apart, a policy of easing such persons out of the world by a completely painless method could appeal to a hardpressed and unsentimental people. But "euthanasia" taught the art of killing and accustomed those who directed and those who administered the death injections to the taking of human life. Once any scruples and inhibitions about killing were overcome and the custom was established, there followed naturally an indifference as to what lives were taken.

Perhaps also those who become involved in any killings are not to be in a good position to decline further requests. If one is convinced that a person should be put out of the way because, from no fault of his own, he has ceased to be a social asset, it is not hard to satisfy the conscience that those who are willful enemies of the prevailing social order have no better right to exist. And so Hadamar drifted from a hospital to a human slaughterhouse.

12

What Is to Be Done?

Despotism may govern without faith, but liberty cannot.[1]

Tocqueville, the nineteenth-century French commentator, was describing the influence of religion on the American republic when he made the above point. We should keep it in mind in deciding what we can do to change the anti-life trends discussed in the preceding chapters.

On one level, we ought to intensify our legislative efforts, primarily for an uncompromising Human Life Amendment. In the interim, it is important to terminate all direct and indirect public funding of abortions, including tax exemptions and privileges for foundations and other organizations which perform or procure abortions. Nor should money that is paid for an abortion be a tax-deductible medical expense. Another legislative initiative is prohibition of experimentation on unborn babies who are slated for abortion and on living or dead victims of deliberate abortions.

It is unrealistic, however, to think that respect for life can be restored merely by dealing with a symptom, legalized abortion. A basic problem is the official establishment of the contraceptive ethic as public policy. The Supreme Court decisions which have brought this about must be reversed, whether by the court itself, implicitly by Congress through withdrawal of the court's jurisdiction, or by the people through the amending process. The objective is to restore to the states and the communities the power to impose reasonable and effective restrictions on such activities as the distribution of contraceptives and the traffic in pornography.

ˑThese and other legislative efforts mentioned in the preceding chapters are important, but they are only part of the program that is needed. On a practical level, private initiatives can do much to relieve the material needs which lead some to favor anti-life policies. Assistance to expectant mothers can save lives, but it should not stop there. Needy families, the retarded, the aged, and others should be the special concern of all churches and various private groups. We cannot look to government to relieve the problems it has helped to create. The decline of the churches' influence, it is fair to say, has been in direct proportion to their willingness to turn their responsibilities over to the state and to become beneficiaries of government handouts.

Besides legislation and practical aid to those who are in need, another priority task is education. The excesses of the godless state do not arise from miscalculation or inefficiency, they occur precisely because the state is godless. God, our Creator and Father, has given us directions, in revelation and the natural moral law, to show us how things work.[2] Neither men nor society can ignore those directions with impunity. We are experiencing the difficulties we have discussed because we have ignored the law of God. We have tried to construct a society without God, and it will not work.

Fortunately, we heed not proceed by guesswork on the application of the law of God to our problems. Christ is God and he teaches through his Vicar on earth. The encyclicals of the popes provide the principles that should govern our policies. *Humanae Vitae,* the hopeful, constructive encyclical of Pope Paul VI on marriage and the generation of life, is of prime importance, and the Catholic bishops would serve the nation well if they would make the dissemination of the truth of *Humanae Vitae* a task of the highest urgency. Too often, the misrepresentations of disloyal or confused theologians are allowed to obscure this truth in the public forum. *Humanae Vitae* is a teaching of the pope, but its relevance is not limited to Catholics. As do the Declaration on Procured Abortion and other teachings of the Church, it explains the principles which are necessary for all men for the attainment of peace and happiness in society.

The objective, in short, must be free acceptance by the American people of the truth of those teachings. The state must be subject to the higher law of God. Nevertheless, we need a visible interpreter with acknowledged moral authority to declare the meaning of that law. In the nature of things, that interpreter has to be the Vicar of Christ. This may appear to be a radical fantasy, but sooner or later the moral bankruptcy of the godless state will be so evident that it will be "respectable" to advocate a radical solution. It must be the Catholic solution.

Beyond any doubt, however, the most important thing we can do is pray. Back in the days before the birth control mentality took hold, Bertrand Russell said that a grave danger faced America—that it would be Catholic in one hundred fifty years. Archbishop Fulton J. Sheen responded that if America "is to be Catholic, it will have to do two more things than it is doing now: It will have to begin to think, and it will have to begin to pray."[3]

All of us, whether Catholic or not, will have to begin to think—about positivism, secularism, the gift of life—and God But most important, we will have to pray. Of ourselves, we can do absolutely nothing, but "nothing shall be impossible with God."[4]

There are some who say that God is dead. In fact, he is not even tired. He is worthy of trust. Whatever happens, we ought to call on him with confidence, particularly through the aid of Mary, his mother.

Notes

Chapter 1

1. *National Catholic Register*, Dec. 1, 1974, p. 1.

2. New York *Times*, May 30, 1975, p. 31, col. 2.

3. *California Medicine*, 113 (Sept. 1970), 67.

4. *Beal v. Doe*, 97 S.Ct. 2366, 2395-96 (1977) (citations omitted).

5. Chicago *Tribune*, Aug. 6, 1977, p. 1, col. 1.

6. For a more powerful and moving portrayal of how the future state might eliminate the "useless aged," see Dale Francis, "The Waiting Room—2020 A.D.," *National Catholic Register*, Jan. 20, 1974, p. 7, col. 1.

Chapter 2

1. Edward S. Corwin, "Constitution vs. Constitutional Theory," 19 *Am. Pol. Sci. Rev.* (1925), 290; see James McClellan, *Joseph Story and the American Constitution* (1971), pp. 112-13.

2. William Kenealy, S.J., "The Majesty of the Law," 5 *Loyola L. Rev.* 101 (1950) (emphasis in original).

3. See discussion in Heinrich Rommen, "Natural Law in Decisions of the Federal Supreme Court and of the Constitutional Courts in Germany," 4 *Natural Law Forum* 1, 11 (1959).

4. Hans Kelsen, *Essays in Legal and Moral Philosophy*, Ota Weinberger, ed. (1973), p. ix.

5. Hans Kelsen, "Absolutism and Relativism in Philosophy and Politics," 42 *Am. Pol. Sci. Review* 906 (1948).

6. Ibid., pp. 913-14.

7. Hans Kelsen, "The Pure Theory of Law, Part II, 51 *"Law Quart. Rev.* (1935), pp. 517, 518-19.

8. Ibid., Part I, 50 *Law Quart. Rev.* (1934), 474.

9. Ernst von Hippel, "The Role of Natural Law in the Legal Decisions of the Federal German Republic, "4 *Natural Law Forum* 106, 107 (1959) (emphasis in original).

10. Ibid., p. 109.

11. Ibid., p. 110.

12. For details, see Leo Alexander, M.D., "Medical Science under Dictatorship," *New England Journal of Medicine* (July 14, 1949), p. 39.

13. Von Hippel, "The Role of Natural Law," pp. 110-11.

14. Heinrich Rommen, "Natural Law in Decisions of the Federal Supreme Court and of the Constitutional Courts in Germany," 4 *Natural Law Forum* 1, 11 (1959).

15. Jeremy Bentham, "Theory of Legislation," in Morris R. Cohen and Felix S. Cohen, eds., *Readings in Jurisprudence and Legal Philosophy* (1951), p. 600.

16. Ibid., p. 601.

17. See Heinrich Rommen, *The Natural Law* (1948), pp. 124-34.

18. See, generally, Alfred J. Ayer, *Language, Truth and Logic* (1952), and *A Modern Introduction to Philosophy*, Paul Edwards and Arthur Pap, eds. (1957), pp. 726-56.

Chapter 3

1. Paul Blanshard and Edd Doerr, "A Glorious Victory," *The Humanist* (May/June 1973), p. 5.

2. *The Humanist* (May/June 1973), p. 3.

3. Gerhart Niemeyer, *The Communist Ideology, Facts on Communism,* (Committee on Un-American Activities, U.S. House of Representatives) (1959), 1:133.

4. Whitaker Chambers, *Cold Friday* (1964), pp. 68–69.

5. Niemeyer, *Communist Ideology*, p. 135.

6. George Orwell, *1984* (1950), pp. 189–90 (emphasis in original).

7. New York *Times,* Aug. 26, 1973, p. 1, col. 3.

8. *The Humanist Frame,* Julian Huxley, ed. (1961), p. 18.

9. Ibid., p. 40.

10. Ibid., p. 351.

11. R. J. Rushdoony, *Chalcedon Report* (Aug. 1, 1972) (Box 158, Vallecito, Calif. 95251).

12. See Vincent P. Miceli, S.J., *The Gods of Atheism* (1971), pp. 198–215.

13. Rushdoony, *Chalcedon Report,* Aug. 1, 1972.

14. St. Louis *Globe Democrat,* Feb. 19, 1977.

15. *L'Osservatore Romano* (English ed.), Mar. 4, 1976, p. 6.

16. In John C. Bennett, *Christianity and Our World* (1943), p. 41.

17. In *The Humanist Frame,* p. 349.

18. See Charles E. Rice, *Authority and Rebellion* (1971) p. 226.

Chapter 4

1. Christopher Derrick, *Escape from Scepticism* (1977), p. 47.

2. Pope Paul VI, allocution, Mar. 12, 1964; AAS 56 (1964).

3. Cornelius Hagerty, C.S.C., *The Problem of Evil* (1978), p. 18.

4. Pope Pius XII, *Humani Generis.*

5. Heinrich Rommen, *The Natural Law* (1948), p. 165.

6. Ibid.

7. See *The Pocket Aquinas,* Vernon Bourke, ed. (1969), pp. 3–5).

8. Aristotle, *Nicomachean Ethics,* book V.

9. Marcus Tullius Cicero, *De Legibus*, II, 5.

10. Ibid., I, 16.

11. Ibid., II, 5.

12. *The Great Legal Philosophers*, Clarence Morris, ed. (1959), p. 42.

13. Anton-Hermann Chroust, "The Philosophy of Law of St. Thomas Aquinas: His Fundamental Ideas and Some of His Historical Precursors," 19 *American Journal of Jurisprudence* (1974), 1, 23.

14. Anton-Hermann Chroust, "The Fundamental Ideas in St. Augustine's Philosophy of Law," 18 *American Journal of Jurisprudence* (1973), 57.

15. Chroust, "The Philosophy of Law of St. Thomas Aquinas," p. 24.

16. St. Thomas Aquinas, *Summa Theologica*, I, II, Q. 91, art. 1.

17. Ibid., art. 4.

18. Ibid., art. 2.

19. Ibid., Q. 94, art. 2.

20. Rommen, *The Natural Law*, p. 50.

21. Aquinas, *Summa Theologica*, I, II, Q. 94, art. 2.

22. See Thomas E. Davitt, S.J., "St. Thomas Aquinas and the Natural Law," in *Origins of the Natural Law Tradition* (1954), pp. 26, 30–31; Rommen, *The Natural Law*, p. 49; Aquinas, *Summa Theologica*, I, II, Q. 94, art. 2.

23. Rommen, *The Natural Law*, pp. 48–49.

24. Aquinas, *Summa Theologica*, I, II, Q. 94, art. 6.

25. Ibid., art. 3, 6.

26. Ibid., Q. 95, art. 2.

27. Ibid.

28. Ibid., Q. 96, art. 1.

29. Ibid., art. 2.

30. Ibid., Q. 95, art. 2.

31. Ibid., Q. 96, art. 4 (emphasis added).

32. Ibid., Q. 90, art. 1.

33. Ibid., Q. 91, art. 1.

34. Rommen, *The Natural Law*, p. 51.

35. Aquinas, *Summa Theologica*, I, II, Q. 96, art. 4.

36. Ibid.

Chapter 5

1. The Declaration of Independence (emphasis added).

2. Edward S. Corwin, "The 'Higher Law' Background of American Constitutional Law," 42 *Harv. L. Rev.* 149, 152 (1928).

3. 8 Coke's Rep., 107(a), 77 Eng. Rep. 638, 652 (1610).

4. Calvin's Case, 7 Coke's Rep., 1(a), 77 Eng. Rep. 377, 392 (1610).

5. See Roscoe Pound, "The Development of Constitutional Guarantees of Liberty," 20 *Notre Dame Law.* (1945), 347, 367.

6. See Clarence Manion, "The Natural Law Philosophy of Founding Fathers," 1 *Natural Law Institute Proceedings* (1947), 3, 11–12.

7. William Blackstone, *Commentaries on the Laws of England* (1765), pp. 160–62.

8. 1 Jefferson's Va. Rep., 109, 114 (1772).

9. Manion, "The Natural Law Philosophy of Founding Fathers," pp. 3, 26 (1947).

10. Ibid., pp. 23–24.

11. Pound, "The Development of Constitutional Guarantees of Liberty," pp. 347, 349.

12. John Locke, *Second Treatise of Civil Government*, II, sec. 123–124.

13. Ibid., sec. 135.

14. Ibid., sec. 149.

15. Ibid., sec. 95–96.

16. Heinrich Rommen, *The Natural Law* (1948), p. 90.

17. Corwin, " 'Higher Law' Background," p. 396.

18. Ibid., p. 388.

19. See the analysis in James McClellan, *Joseph Story and the Constitution* (1971), pp. 70–81.

Chapter 6

1. *Sierra Club* v. *Morton,* 405 U.S. 727, 742–55 (1972).

2. Holmes, *The Natural Law: Collected Legal Papers* (1920), p. 310.

3. Holmes-Pollock letters (1942), 2:22.

4. *American Banana Co.* v. *United Fruit Co.,* 213 U.S. 347, 356 (1909); see William J. Kenealy, S.J., "The Majesty of the Law," 5 *Loyola Law Rev.* 101, 107 (1950).

5. *Holmes–Pollock Letters,* 2:36.

6. Ibid., p. 252.

7. Thomas Cooley, *Constitutional Limitations* (3rd ed., 1874), p. 168.

8. *Korematsu* v. *U.S.,* 323 U.S. 214 (1944).

9. *Lochner* v. *New York,* 198 U.S. 45 (1905).

10. *NAACP* v. *Alabama,* 357 U.S. 449 (1957).

11. *Griswold* v. *Connecticut,* 381 U.S. 479 (1965).

12. Ernst von Hippel, "The Role of Natural Law in the Legal Decisions of the German Federal Republic," *Natural Law Forum* (1959), p. 106 (emphasis added).

13. Ibid., p. 111.

14. *Byrn* v. *New York City Health and Hospitals Corp.,* 31 N.Y. 2d 194, 335 N.Y.S. 2d 390, 393 (1972), *appeal dismissed,* 410 U.S. 949 (1973).

15. Raoul Berger, "The Imperial Court," *New York Times Magazine,* Oct. 9, 1977, p. 38; see generally, Raoul Berger, "Government by Judiciary" (1977).

16. Morris R. Cohen and Felix S. Cohen, eds., *Readings in Jurisprudence and Legal Philosophy* (1951), p. 552.

17. See discussion in Ben W. Palmer, "The Natural Law and Pragmatism," 1 *Nat. Law Inst. Proceedings* (1947), 30, 35–36.

18. J. Mitchell Morse, "Nothing Is True, Nothing Is False," *Chronicle of Higher Education* (Apr. 5, 1976), p. 40.

19. *Gertz* v. *Welch,* 418 U.S. 323, 339 (1974).

20. *Gitlow* v. *N.Y.* 268 U.S. 652, 673 (1925).

21. *Robin* v. *Hardaway,* 1 Jefferson's Va. Rep., 109, 114 (1772).

22. United States Commission on Civil Rights, *Constitutional Aspects of the Right to Limit Childbearing* (1975), p. 1.

23. Ibid., p. 79.

24. Pope Pius XII, allocution, "Magnificate Dominum" (1954).

25. Second Vatican Council, Declaration on Religious Freedom, no. 14.

26. George Otto Trevelyan, *The Life and Letters of Lord Macaulay*, 2:409 ff. (1876); quoted in *Chalcedon Report* (Jan. 1973), p. 2.

Chapter 7

1. *Torcaso* v. *Watkins*, 367 U.S. 488, 490 (1961).

2. 367 U.S. at 495.

3. See Clarence Manion, *Cancer in the Constitution* (1972).

4. Definitive Treaty of Peace between the United States of America and His Britannic Majesty, Sept. 3, 1783, 8 Statutes 80.

5. Douglas Southall Freeman, *George Washington* (1954), VI, 196–97.

6. *Annals of Congress,* I, 949.

7. Thomas Cooley, *Principles of Constitutional Law* (1898), p. 224.

8. Joseph Story, *Commentaries on the Constitution of the United States* (1891), sec. 1874, 1877.

9. 143 U.S. 457, 470–71 (1892). (Emphasis added).

10. *Davis* v. *Beason*, 133 U.S. 333, 342 (1890).

11. 370 U.S. 421 (1962).

12. *Abington School District* v. *Schempp*, 374 U.S. 203 (1963).

13. 374 U.S. at 220.

14. 374 U.S. at 303–4. (Emphasis added).

15. *Stein* v. *Oshinsky*, 348 F.2d 999 (2d Cir., 1965) *cert. denied*, 382 U.S. 957 (1965).

16. *DeSpain* v. *DeKalb County Community School Dist.* 384 F.2d 836 (1967), *cert. denied*, 390 U.S. 906 (1968).

17. *State Bd. of Educ.* v. *Bd. of Educ. of Netcong*, 108 N.J. Super. 564, 262 A. 2d 21, *aff'd*, 57 N.J. 172, 270 A. 2d 412 (1970), *cert. denied*, 401 U.S. 1013 (1971).

18. 374 U.S. at 239–40.

19. *Catholic Currents*, Nov. 15, 1971, p. 3.

20. See New York *Times*, Aug. 24, 1977 p. 6, col. 1.

21. Ibid., Dec. 8, 1977, p. A18, col. 1.

22. Declaration on Christian Education, no. 3 (emphasis added).

23. Pope Pius XI, *Quadragesimo Anno* (1931).

24. Declaration on Christian Education, no. 3.

25. *Complete Works of Lincoln*, Nicolay and Hay, eds., (1905), VIII, 235.

Chapter 8

1. New York *Times*, July 24, 1977, p. 1, col. 1.

2. *U.S. News & World Report*, Aug. 8, 1977, p. 54.

3. New York *Times*, Feb. 6, 1977, p. 1, col. 1.

4. Ibid., Oct. 19, 1977, p. 1, col. 2.

5. Ibid., May 22, 1977, p. E7, col. 5.

6. Ibid., Oct. 10, 1976, p. 59, col. 1.

7. Ibid., May 22, 1977, p. E7, col. 4.

8. South Bend (Ind.) *Tribune*, May 22, 1977, p. 16, col. 1.

9. *Our Sunday Visitor* (news ed.), June 26, 1977, p. 4, col. 4.

10. *The Harmonizer* (Huntington, Ind.), Dec .1, 1977, p. 1, col. 1.

11. New York *Times*, Oct. 9, 1975, p. 1, col. 1.

12. Second Vatican Council, *Lumen Gentium* (The Dogmatic Constitution on the Church), no. 25.

13. See, generally, Edwin F. Healy, S.J., *Moral Guidance* (1960), pp. 24–27; John A. Hardon, S.J., *The Catholic Catechism* (1974), pp. 290–93.

14. Pope Paul VI, *Humanae Vitae*.

15. For information, contact Human Life Center, St. John's University, Collegeville, Minn. 56321.

16. *Coverline* (Box 250, New Haven, Conn. 06502; Summer 1973) (emphasis in original).

17. Elizabeth B. Connell, M.D., "The Search for an Ideal Contraceptive, "*Medical Opinion* (Feb. 1977), p. 10.

18. Boston *Sunday Globe, New England Magazine,* Aug. 21, 1977, p. 18.

19. *National Catholic Register,* Sept. 12, 1976, p. 1, col. 2.

20. Anthony Harrigan, in *U.S. Industrial Council* (column), Nov. 4, 1976.

21. South Bend (Ind.) *Tribune,* May 26, 1977, p. 11, col. 2.

22. *Family Planning News,* Sept. 1, 1975.

23. New York *Times,* Jan. 1, 1977, p. 4, col. 7.

24. *Vital Statistics Report* (National Center for Health Statistics), Mar. 8, 1977.

25. "Conversations with Pope Paul VI, *"McCall's,* Oct. 1967.

26. Newark *Star-Ledger,* Oct. 15, 1970; *The Wanderer,* Oct. 9, 1975, p. 2, col. 1.

27. *The Late Corp. of the Church of Jesus Christ of Latter-Day Saints* v. *U.S.,* 136 U.S. 1, 49 (1890); see John T. Noonan Jr., "The Family and the Supreme Court," 23 *Catholic Univ. L. Rev.* 255 (1973).

28. *Pierce* v. *Society of Sisters,* 268 U.S. 510, 535 (1925).

29. 381 U.S. 479, 484 (1965).

30. 405 U.S. 438, 453 (1972).

31. Pope John XXIII, *Pacem in Terris,* n. 16.

32. 428 U.S. 52 (1976).

33. 97 S. Ct. 2010, 2017 (1977).

34. *Moore* v. *City of East Cleveland, Ohio,* 97 S. Ct. 1932, 1938 (1977).

35. 136 U.S. at 49.

36. Albert V. Dicey, *Law and Public Opinion in England* (1926), p. 469; Charles E. Rice, *Freedom of Association* (1962), pp. 15–16.

37. James Zatko, *Descent into Darkness: The Destruction of the Roman Catholic Church in Russia, 1917–1923* (1965), p. 73.

Chapter 9

1. *The Harmonizer* (Huntington, Ind.), June 26, 1977, p. 4, col. 4.

2. *U.S. News & World Report*, Nov. 13, 1972, p. 28.

3. Chicago *Tribune*, Dec. 11, 1976, sec. 1, p. 8, col. 1.

4. *Abortion Research Notes* (International Reference Center for Abortion Research), Feb. 1977, p. 7; New York *Times*, Oct. 26, 1977, p. 44, col. 1.

5. New York *Times*, June 28, 1972, p. 1, col. 3.

6. See Leslie Arey, *Developmental Anatomy* (1954); Dr. and Mrs. J. C. Willke, *Handbook on Abortion* (1971); *Newsweek*, Oct. 25, 1965, p. 67; Bart T. Heffernan, M.D., "The Early Biography of Everyman," in *Abortion and Social Justice*, Thomas W. Hilgers, M.D., and Dennis Horan, eds. (1972), p. 3; Geraldine Flanagan, *The First Nine Months of Life* (1965).

7. See *Fetology: The Smallest Patients, The Sciences* (New York Academy of Sciences), Oct. 1968; New York *Times*, Apr. 7, 1973, p. 14, col. 5.

8. Bradley M. Patten, *Human Embryology* (1953), p. 54 (emphasis in original).

9. New York *Times*, Mar. 9, 1977, p. 25, col. 1.

10. *Legislative Services*, (U.S. Coalition for Life), Oct. 1977.

11. See *U.S.* v. *Holmes*, 26 F. Cas. 360 (no. 15, 383) (C.C.E.D. Pa., 1842); *Regina* v. *Dudley*, 14 Q.B.D. 273, 15 Cox Crim. Cas. 624 (1884); see, generally, F. Inbau, J. Thompson, and C. Sowle, *Criminal Justice* (1968), pp. 14–15; Jerome Hall, *General Principles of Criminal Law* (1947), pp. 422–23.

12. Ethical and Religious Directives for Catholic Health Facilities, para. 16; see para. 17 governing removal of the womb.

13. John A. Hardon, S.J., *The Catholic Catechism* (1975), p. 337.

14. Rev. Donald McCarthy, Ph.D., "Medication to Prevent Pregnancy after Rape" and William A. Lynch, M.D., "Comments on Medication to Prevent Pregnancy after Rape," both in *Linacre Quarterly*, (Aug. 1977), 210, 223.

15. New York *Times*, May 12, 1976, p. 37, col. 5.

16. See Thomas W. Hilgers, M.D., "The Medical Hazards of Legally Induced Abortion," in *Abortion and Social Justice*, p. 57.

17. New York *Times*, May 14, 1976, p. A27, col. 4.

18. See discussion in Colorado Right to Life Committee *Newsletter*, Nov. 11, 1975.

19. Ibid., June 1976, p. 9.

20. See editorial, *The New Republic*, July 2, 1977, pp. 5-6; *Newsletter* (Christian Anti-Communism Crusade), Aug. 1, 1977, p. 8.

21. Alan Guttmacher, M.D., "Techniques of Therapeutic Abortion," *Clinical Obstetrics and Gynecology* (Mar. 1964), pp. 100, 103.

22. See *Abortion and Social Justice*, pp. 291-93.

23. Chicago *Tribune*, June 3, 1972.

24. *Medical World News*, Dec. 1, 1975; Arlene Doyle, "The Abortion Mentality: How It Conditions Us," *The Wanderer*, Jan. 22, 1976, p. 4, col. 1; see Chicago *Tribune*, Aug. 11, 1976, p. 1, col. 1.

25. *Human Life Newsletter* (Seattle), Nov.-Dec. 1976.

Chapter 10

1. 410 U.S. 113 (1973).

2. 410 U.S. 179 (1973).

3. See Note, "The Law and the Unborn Child: The Legal and Logical Inconsistencies," vol. 46, *Notre Dame Lawyer* (1971), p. 349.

4. *Scott* v. *Sandford*, 15 L. Ed. 691, 709, 720 (1857).

5. See, generally, Alfred Avins, *The Reconstruction Amendment Debates* (1967).

6. 410 U.S. at 157, fn. 54.

7. *Sendak* v. *Arnold*, 97 S. Ct. 476 (1976).

8. 410 U.S. at 164.

9. 410 U.S. at 163.

10. 410 U.S. at 160.

11. 410 U.S. at 164.

12. *Doe* v. *Bolton*, 410 U.S. at 191-92.

13. 428 U.S. 52 (1976).

14. 428 U.S. at 82.

15. 428 U.S. at 83.

16. *Beal* v. *Doe*, 97 S. Ct. 2366 (1977); *Maher* v. *Roe*, 97 S. Ct. 2376 (1977).

17. *Poelker* v. *Doe*, 97 S. Ct. 239 (1977).

18. *Ex parte McCardle*, 19 L. Ed. 264 (1868).

19. Sacred Congregation for the Doctrine of the Faith, Declaration on Procured Abortion (1974), no. 21–22.

20. 410 U.S. at 161.

21. Geraldine Flanagan, The First Nine Months of Life (1965), 35.

22. H. J. Res. 681, 94th Cong.

23. S.J. Res. 15, 95th Cong., 1st sess.

24. See the definition of fetus in *Dorland's Medical Dictionary* (21st ed.).

25. See Harriet Pilpel, "The Collateral Legal Consequences of Adopting a Constitutional Amendment on Abortion, *"Family Planning/ Population Reporter* (June 1976).

26. Germain Grisez, *Abortion: The Myths, the Realities and the Arguments* (1970), pp. 78-81.

27. S.J. Res. 6, 95th Cong., 1st sess.

28. For example, an amendment would appear to ensure protection to the unborn child at every stage of pregnancy if it were phrased according to the suggestion of Dean-Emeritus Joseph O'Meara of the Notre Dame Law School: "With respect to the right to life guaranteed by this Constitution, an unborn is a person at every stage of biological development." (See Joseph O'Meara, "The Demise of the Supreme Court" (1978).

29. *The Harmonizer*, (Huntington, Ind.), Oct. 9, 1977, p. 1, col. 1.

30. *Casti Connubii*, Dec. 31, 1930.

31. Grisez, *Abortion*, p. 349.

32. Sacred Congregation for the Doctrine of the Faith, Declaration on Procured Abortion (1974), no. 13, quoting Tertullian, *Apologeticum*.

33. Second Vatican Council, *Gaudium et Spes* (Pastoral Constitution on the Church in the Modern World), no. 51.

34. See Dr. and Mrs. J. C. Willke, *Handbook on Abortion* (1971), p. 92.

35. 97 S. Ct. at 2399.

36. Leo Alexander, M.D., "Medical Science Under Dictatorship," *New England Journal of Medicine* (July 14, 1949), p. 39.

37. *National Catholic Register,* Oct. 30, 1977, p. 1, col. 5.

Chapter 11

1. Washington *Post,* Aug. 26, 1977, p. A18, col. 1.

2. *U.S. News & World Report,* Oct. 3, 1977, p. 54.

3. See *Smith* v. *Smith,* 229 Ark. 579, 317 S.W. 2d 275, 279 (1958); *Thomas* v. *Anderson,* 96 Cal. App 2d 371, 215 P.2d 478, 481 (1950).

4. Frank J. Ayd Jr., M.D., "What Is Death?" *Medical-Moral Newsletter* (Oct. 1968).

5. Matter of Quinlan, 355 A.2d 647, 654–55 (1976).

6. New York *Times,* Aug. 5, 1968, p. 1, col. 6.

7. See "Annotation, Tests of Death for Organ Transplant Purposes," 76 A. L. R. 3d 913 (1977).

8. New York *Times,* Dec. 5, 1976, p. 26, col. 1.

9. *Respect Life!* (National Conference of Catholic Bishops), June 14, 1977.

10. South Bend (Ind.), *Tribune,* June 15, 1977, p. 16, col. 3.

11. See Dennis J. Horan, "The 'Right to Die': Legislative and Judicial Developments," address to Medicine and Law Committee, American Bar Assn., Aug. 9, 1977.

12. Michael Garland, "Politics, Legislation and Natural Death, *"Hastings Center Report,* Oct. 19, 1976, p. 6.

13. Matter of Quinlan, 355 A2d 647, 655 (1976).

14. *Superintendent of Belcherton State School* v. *Saikewicz,* Nov. 29, 1977, 370 N.E. 2d 417 (Mass. Supreme Judicial Court, 1977).

15. New York *Times,* Apr. 2, 1976, p. 30, col. 2.

16. 355 A.2d at 656.

17. See also *Superintendent of Belcherton State School* v. *Saikewicz,* 370 N.E.2d417 (Mass., 1977)

18. *National Catholic Register,* Oct. 31, 1971, p. 2, col. 1.

19. R. S. Duff and A. G. M. Campbell, "Moral and Ethical Dilemmas in the Special Care Nursery," *New England Journal of Medicine* (Oct. 25, 1973), p. 890, C. Everett Koop, M.D., The Right To Live, The Right To Die (1976), p. 90.

20. See Robert M. Byrn, "Compulsory Lifesaving Treatment for the Competent Adult," 44 *Fordham L. Rev.* 1 (1975).

21. See, generally, Frederick Wertham, M.D., *A Sign for Cain* (1966); Leo Alexander, M.D., "Medical Science under Dictatorship," *New England Journal of Medicine* (July 14, 1949), p. 39.

22. Calvin J. Frederick, M.D., in *Current Trends in Suicidal Behavior in the United States* (May 1, 1977), p. 13. Dr. Frederick is chief of the Mental Health Disaster Assistance Section of the National Institute of Mental Health.

23. *Our Sunday Visitor* (news ed.), Jan. 9, 1977, p. 2, col. 1.

24. H.B. 2614, Legislature of the State of Florida, prefiled July 1971.

Chapter 12

1. Alexis de Tocqueville, *Democracy in America* (1959), I, 318.

2. See Edward J. Murphy, *Life to the Full* (Our Sunday Visitor Press, 1978).

3. Fulton J. Sheen, *Moods and Truths* (1932), p. 191.

4. Lk 1:37.

Index

(continued from page ii)

lative efforts must be stepped up, concentrating on an uncompromising human life amendment. It is unrealistic, however, to think that respect for life can be restored merely by dealing with a symptom, legalized abortion. A basic problem is the official establishment of contraceptive ethic as public policy. Essentially, the key is awakening an awareness of and educating to counteract the dangerous trend towards total secularization. We cannot look to government to relieve the problems it has helped to create. The decline of the churches' influence, it is fair to say, has been in direct proportion to their willingness to turn their responsibilities over to the state and to become beneficiaries of government handouts.

Readable and concise, not burdened by a heavy, legalistic style, this book is useful as a summary of the abortion situation in general and excellent as a handbook for concerned individuals. All of us, whether Catholic or not, have to begin to think—about positivism, secularism, the gift of life—and God.

CHARLES E. RICE is a professor of law at University of Notre Dame Law School and editor of the American Journal of Jurisprudence.

5259

ISBN 0-8199-0696-4
Jacket Design by William Dichtl
Made in the United States of America